Praise for

There's a Woman in the Pulpit
Christian Clergywomen Share Their Hard Days, Holy Moments & the Healing Power of Humor

"My neck and throat are sore after reading this book; my neck from nodding all the way through and my throat from laughing out loud. *There's a Woman in the Pulpit* offers a circle of witness for women pastors and a universal message of joy and hope. A great gift for us all!"

—**Rev. Susan Sparks**, pastor, Madison Avenue Baptist Church, New York City; author, *Laugh Your Way to Grace: Reclaiming the Spiritual Power of Humor*

"Once again Martha Spong and RevGalBlogPals ... have found a way to strengthen women in their ministries and to do so with transparency, poignancy and wit. Whether you are a woman in ministry or know a woman in ministry, these stories will touch your soul and intensify your own faith and faithfulness."

—**Jenee Woodard**, curator, The Text This Week (www.textweek.com)

"For many pastors, the practice of ministry can be lonely at times. But this fantastic book made me feel like I was sitting with my girlfriends, honestly discussing both the beauty and pain of being a woman in the pulpit. To say that I could identify with most of the stories would be an understatement. I am so thankful for their courage to give voice to our experience!"

—**Rev. Shannon J. Kershner**, pastor, Fourth Presbyterian Church, Chicago

"Refreshingly down-to-earth humor.... These preachers welcome us into their callings and into their lives [and] send us out again encouraged and renewed for the work and life ahead."

—**Rev. Dr. David J. Lose**, president, Lutheran Theological Seminary at Philadelphia; founder, WorkingPreacher.org; blogger, In the Meantime (davidlose.net)

"Reading these brief reminiscences of lives lived in ministry to others, I laughed and cried and marveled and knew that I was standing on holy ground. These stories and poems are like well-polished gems. Each is so real and so immediate that, even though it is no more than two or three pages, I feel that I know these women and what a blessing they are to those whose lives they touch. Next time I wonder why I teach in a seminary where we prepare people to minister to God's people, I will pick up this book and remember that I, too, have been called."

—**Deborah Sokolove**, director, Henry Luce III Center for the Arts and Religion; coauthor, *Calling on God: Inclusive Christian Prayers for Three Years of Sundays*

"Lyrical, grace-filled, brutally honest.... Resonate[s] with depth and authenticity that call us back to the messy, beautiful gift of faith community. Don't miss it."

—**Rev. Dr. Amy K. Butler**, senior minister, Riverside Church, New York City

"Vital.... [A] treasure trove of wisdom and grace."

—**Landon Whitsitt**, executive, PCUSA Synod of Mid-America; author, *Open Source Church: Making Room for the Wisdom of All*; producer, *Theocademy*

"Seeps with stories and humor that remind each of us that we are not alone and that we can love our roles and our people."

—**Rev. Jeremy Smith**, United Methodist pastor, Portland, Oregon; blogger, HackingChristianity.net

"Touching, insightful, funny, marvelous."

—**Mary E. Hunt, PhD**, Women's Alliance for Theology, Ethics and Ritual (WATER); coeditor, *New Feminist Christianity: Many Voices, Many Views*

THERE'S A
WOMAN
IN THE PULPIT

Christian Clergywomen
Share Their Hard Days,
Holy Moments &
the Healing
Power of
Humor

EDITED BY REV. MARTHA SPONG

FOREWORD BY REV. CAROL HOWARD MERRITT

CHRISTIAN JOURNEYS

FROM SKYLIGHT PATHS® PUBLISHING

Woodstock, Vermont

There's a Woman in the Pulpit:
Christian Clergywomen Share Their Hard Days, Holy Moments and the Healing Power of Humor

2015 Quality Paperback Edition, First Printing
© 2015 by Martha Spong
Foreword © 2015 by Carol Howard Merritt

Library of Congress Cataloging-in-Publication Data
There's a woman in the pulpit : Christian clergywomen share their hard days, holy moments and the healing power of humor / edited by Rev. Martha Spong ; foreword by Rev. Carol Howard.
  pages cm
 ISBN 978-1-59473-588-2 (pbk.)
 1. Women clergy. I. Spong, Martha 1961– editor.
 BV676.T4925 2015
 253.082—dc23
                    2015001609
ISBN 978-1-59473-603-2 (eBook)

10 9 8 7 6 5 4 3 2 1

Manufactured in the United States of America
Cover design: Jenny Buono
Cover art: © Cienpies Design / Shutterstock.com
Interior design: Tim Holtz

SkyLight Paths Publishing is creating a place where people of different spiritual traditions come together for challenge and inspiration, a place where we can help each other understand the mystery that lies at the heart of our existence.

SkyLight Paths sees both believers and seekers as a community that increasingly transcends traditional boundaries of religion and denomination—people wanting to learn from each other, *walking together, finding the way.*

SkyLight Paths, "Walking Together, Finding the Way" and colophon are trademarks of LongHill Partners, Inc., registered in the U.S. Patent and Trademark Office.

Walking Together, Finding the Way®
Published by SkyLight Paths Publishing
A Division of LongHill Partners, Inc.
Sunset Farm Offices, Route 4, P.O. Box 237
Woodstock, VT 05091
Tel: (802) 457-4000 Fax: (802) 457-4004

Contents

A Taste of Heaven and a Splash of Glory   37
Sharing the Sacraments

Ashes to Angels   75
Ministry and Death

They Don't Teach That in Seminary   103
What We Learned Through Experience

It's Complicated   141
Being Pastor/Partner/Parent/Person

Outside Over There   175
Moving in the World Beyond Our Churches

Foreword

I had just finished leading worship. I was standing at the receiving end of the postservice handshake queue when another clergywoman glanced at the back of my robe and burst into laughter. With her forefinger, she traced a thin white drip that stretched from my shoulder to five inches down my back. She saw the line and quickly filled in the backstory. Once I also realized what she was pointing out, my chuckling voice rose to meet hers. There were few people on the planet who would know about that telltale line, but she had just the right understanding of the sacred/ordinary balancing act in which we were caught up. I had baby puke on my preaching garb.

I had stolen a few minutes before the service to breast-feed my infant, Calla. When I was done, I quickly put on my robe. Without thinking, I placed my daughter's tiny chin on the padded left shoulder. I moved my fingers up and down the small bumps of her spine, smelled her scalp, patted her back, and burped her. I wanted to make sure that her tummy was full and free of gas before I handed her off to the church grandmothers in the pews. It was always easier to preach when I knew my daughter was satisfied.

The only problem with my Sunday morning routine was that I forgot to look over my shoulder for the remains of her breakfast. After the handshake line cleared, I went back to my office. I shrugged off my black academic preaching robe and blotted the baby spittle with a wet wipe. The juxtaposition of that dark garb, a cultural designation to remind the congregation of my intellectual capacity, decorated with a line of infant vomit, reminded me of how lucky I was. Women have always found ways to minister, with or without credentialing, but I have had the chance to fully live into that calling. I am in a rich, ripe moment of history, where I don't have to fight for my right to be in the pulpit (at least, not after I changed denominations), but I can fully minister as an ordained pastor, with all the blessings from the institution. When I felt satisfied with the faded line, I hung up the robe and went to find my infant in the swarm of people eating cookies in the fellowship hall.

Calla reached for me and I took her in my arms as I listened to pastoral care concerns. A man was going into surgery. A grandmother was worried about her grandson. Someone had lost his job. I listened as I shifted my daughter from hip to hip. I promised prayers as I held her close.

In ministry, we constantly balance the sacred and the ordinary, juggling the two as expertly as we manage a chalice and a bottle. Even as we do things as simple as lighting the candles, setting the table, breaking the bread, and pouring the wine, we invite people into a holy moment. As the smell of smoke fills the air and that bread sticks to the roof of our mouths, we remember the marvel of being fed.

We consume the food, allowing ourselves to taste it. Setting aside the ravenous appetite that we will bring to the Sunday all-you-can-eat brunch buffet, we let this bite linger on our tongue, digesting the full knowledge that we can find something holy in our ordinary acts. We become attentive to the wonder of everyday life as we share a morsel that unites us with people all over the world.

This ordinary bread and wine does not become holy because it is qualitatively better than the bread found on our tables, but because they are somehow set apart. Through communion, we wake people up to the sense of the sacredness that infuses every table.

As women of the cloth, we have many places where we can be holy and set apart; most of us do not have to fight to be recognized in that manner anymore. But we don't have many spaces where we can be ordinary. We were taught the beauty of liturgy, the nuances of preaching, and the presence of ministry, but we were not always taught what to do to get the baby spit off our preaching robe. There are so many things that ordinary holy women have to worry about. What do we wear to wedding receptions now? Or what to do when our most dedicated layperson won't quit staring at our breasts?

It is at this intersection that we can always find the RevGals, the online community from which this book grew. They have been a lifeline to all of us who juggle the sacred and the ordinary. They are women who are never too uptight to joke, "Does this pulpit make my butt look big?" These women not only have a wellspring of deep wisdom, but they also have the ability to dish out their knowledge with side-aching humor.

I have been part of the RevGals community for a decade. They have supported me in times of loneliness. They have encouraged me in despair. They have surrounded me in all the laughter and pain of this holy and ordinary life. And now I am thrilled that their great wisdom and intelligence will be bound into the pages that I can turn to, lend, and appreciate for years to come.

Rev. Carol Howard Merritt
author, *Tribal Church*
carolhowardmerritt.org

Introduction

When I first considered going to seminary, I didn't know any female pastors. Many of the writers in this book have been pioneers: we've left the churches of our childhoods to follow Jesus, and although some of our denominations have ordained women for many years, we've still been the first woman to serve a particular church, or the first single woman, or the first mom, or the first soccer mom. Like many women pursuing historically male professions, we grapple with expectations for our personal lives as well as our vocations in a field where those personal lives are on view as soon as we bring our families to church with us.

Not all women in ministry approach their calling in the same way. Some consider all the possibilities carefully before reaching a conclusion, while others jump in and trust God to catch them in case of disaster. Some react from the heart, while others excel at practical solutions. All learn from experience. And in our stories you will see the Holy Spirit at work, getting us ready for what may come next, honing our skills and our souls to make us better pastors. You will see that we take our callings seriously, but we are also not afraid to find the humor in our lives and our ministry.

You may have picked up this book because you are curious to find out what life at the pastor's house is like. You may be hoping for insight into the joys and struggles of a clergywoman you know and love. You may be considering a call to ordained ministry. You may be a pastor who longs to know that others understand this strange life you lead. We hope you will discover that behind the parsonage door is a real person who loves God and *you* and is willing to work hard to meet the challenges that come with this demanding but rewarding vocation. Whatever your life situation, these stories of the varied ways we answer God's call on our lives will inspire you to listen for the calling that might be welling up within you, and to answer it with every bit of your heart, mind, spirit—and personality.

Our book begins with stories of being called to ministry and learning to lead in the local church. It goes on to explore ministering through the sacraments, being present at the time of death, and the catchall of things we did not learn from the books we read in seminary. The final sections of the book take you into our personal lives, where we share our hopes and disappointments, what we learned from running or learning to belly-dance, as well as what the wider world sees when a clergywoman also teaches water aerobics or writes romance novels. Some stories have a uniquely feminine perspective, while others show that a clergywoman has the same viewpoint any pastor might.

The fifty-two clergywomen whose stories appear in this book represent fifteen denominations: American Baptist Churches; Anglican Church of Aotearoa, New Zealand, and Polynesia; Anglican Church of Canada; Christian Church (Disciples of Christ); Church of England; Church of Scotland; Cooperative Baptist Fellowship; Episcopal Church; Evangelical Lutheran Church in America; Mennonite Church USA; Presbyterian Church (USA); United Church of Canada; United Church of Christ; United Methodist Church; and Universal Fellowship of Metropolitan Community Churches. (Whenever a contributor is described as working for a Presbyterian or Lutheran church, those churches are PCUSA and ELCA.) We follow God's call in the United States, Canada, England, Scotland, and New Zealand.

Our churches are large and small, liturgical and not, rural and urban and suburban. Some of us get paid on time, but others worry whether the check is coming every month and some need another job to put dinner on the table and keep a roof overhead. We serve God outside the local church as chaplains, in specialized ministries, and through our writing. We offer our prayers for God to break through and for people to hear the good news of grace and mercy we share—or just for them to stop calling us at home late on a Saturday night. We tell stories of people we have known, but no real names are used for church members, and some are composites.

This book arose from an online community, where a few dozen women bloggers coalesced around our common work as pastors. Those dozens now reach into the thousands. From the beginning, we determined that, despite differences of theology, practice, and life circumstances, our belief that God calls women to ordained ministry is the common ground on which we stand. For this reason, you will not find theological arguments in this book, but you will find different approaches to and language for what we do in ministry, and for baptism and communion in particular. Our community includes people who are single and married and partnered and divorced and widowed, gay and straight, cis- and transgender, parents and not, clergy and clergy spouses and laypeople, with an age range of twenty-something to seventy-something, from all the denominations and countries mentioned above and more.

RevGalBlogPals began as a volunteer-driven collaborative ministry; guiding its ministry is now my calling. I am one part social media minister, one part technical support, one part cruise director, and one part visionary—less for the modest stipend and more for love. I am delighted to share the voices I have known for years with a wider audience, to show the originality and brilliance and faithfulness of women who continue to answer God's call.

Rev. Martha Spong
director, RevGalBlogPals
revgalblogpals.org

Fierce and Fabulous for Jesus

God's Calling and Our Identity

Then I heard the voice of the Lord saying,
"Whom shall I send, and who will go for us?"
And I said, "Here am I; send me!"

ISAIAH 6:8

Ever since the first woman was ordained to Christian ministry, people have been arguing about what to call her. If the male priest is Father, is the female priest (not priestess) Mother? What if all your male colleagues are Mister or Reverend or Doctor, but you live in the South and the children are told to call you Miss Martha? How do you make sure the church and the community will accept you as the pastor?

Some people watch how we do our jobs in a way they do not watch our male colleagues. Maybe they watch us because they aren't sure about

1

having a woman of any description as pastor. Maybe we watch ourselves because we finally get to live our calling even as we remember that the church we grew up in wouldn't honor it.

It's happened to a lot of clergywomen. We pick up the phone at church, and the caller, hearing a woman's voice, assumes he is speaking to the secretary and asks when the minister will be back. We know assumptions are made based not only on how we sound, but also on what we wear and who we love and how we lead. We work to challenge those assumptions by our public presence, the way we carry ourselves, and the words we choose as we respond. We learn to love on Christ's behalf even in the presence of anger or fear.

These are our stories of responding when God called us to ministry and learning to live through it when the call is not easy. There's only one thing to do when people question your pastoral authority. Go and be who God called you to be, and have no fear, because you are doing it not just for yourself, but also for Jesus. Be fully yourself, whether that means OPI's I'm-Not-Really-a-Waitress-red nails or an immaculate French manicure, a quiet pastoral presence or a fiery prophetic witness.

Or, as a dear pal of the RevGals once advised, whoever you are and wherever God sends you, "Be fierce and fabulous for Jesus."

Swinging

Rev. Ruth Everhart

Late June, 1994

Our swing chairs stir in the slightest breeze, even when the air hangs as still and sticky as corn silk. The chairs' movement seems to be propelled by the cornfields that surround the house. The growing crop creates an almost audible whoosh of exhaled oxygen, a greeny respiration fueled by the withered remains of last year's cornstalks.

To me, the swing chairs were a double surprise. First, that my husband ordered them, as thrifty as he is. Second, that he put large eye-hooks into the porch ceiling to hang them. This house is church-owned and governed by committee.

"If anyone complains," Doug said, as he screwed in the eye-hooks, "screw *them!*"

The swings are made of heavy green cloth and black straps. Wooden poles fit into the straps in an ingenious design that keeps the bucket-like seats spread open. I understand their appeal: a person could belong in one of those chairs.

Rev. Ruth Everhart is a Presbyterian minister and author living in Metro Washington, D.C. She has served three churches, including the Rock Creek Presbyterian Church in central Illinois, which is the setting of this story. Ruth is the author of *Chasing the Divine in the Holy Land*, which takes the reader along on a pilgrimage to Israel and Palestine. Her blog, Love the Work (Do the Work), covers the writing life, church leadership, and travel (rutheverhart.com). She is at work on a spiritual memoir.

3

One Saturday afternoon all four of us are on the porch. It's almost naptime. Doug is reading Dr. Seuss books aloud, with both girls in his lap. We glance up to make sure the eye-hook will hold all of them. I half-listen to my husband's sonorous voice reading *Horton Hatches the Egg* as I think about the next day's sermon.

When the mail truck passes, I walk down the long gravel driveway. Inside the mailbox is a heavy envelope from my mother. By the time I've returned to the porch, I have guessed what it contains.

Doug stops reading as I plunk into the other swing chair and open the envelope. Clippings fall into my lap. An article tells how the Christian Reformed Church—the denomination I grew up in, the one I left in order to be ordained—has voted to disallow women to be ordained as elders or ministers. *Disallow.*

A large full-color picture shows three women wiping their eyes, their faces grim. Each woman wears a white dove pinned to her blouse, a yellow ribbon trailing. It takes me a moment to recognize the contorted faces, but the woman on the far left is my mother.

I put the paper down, my own tears stirred by the sight of my mother's. Would she decide to leave the denomination now, as I had done? I feel an anticipatory grief, knowing how hard that will be for her. Tears escape my eyes.

My daughters climb out of their dad's lap and crowd me. "What's wrong, Mommy? What's wrong?" Their eyes well with tears as they study my face.

The tears of the mothers, I think, visited on the next generation.

Doug has gotten out of the chair too. "Is someone sick?"

"Just the goddamn denomination!"

"Mommy!" My daughters' faces darken in distress. This isn't how their mother talks.

I have to explain. I lean my head back against the green cloth and watch the circling movement of the chair's hook. I listen to it creak as if it's complaining. When I'm calm, I say, "I'm mad because some people don't think women should be ministers."

My daughters' eyebrows draw down into furious Vs. Clara—not yet five—stands up straight and thrusts out her chest. "But you're very good." She says this the way I do after she picks up her toys. Hannah—who just finished first grade—puts her hands on her hips. "Even a first grader knows you're a good minister. Stupid-heads!"

Doug plants a kiss on the top of my head. "Hannah's right. They're stupid-heads!"

He gently pushes my chair and the three of them pass me between them. As I go around in a circle, I look up again at the transgressive hardware. My husband was right to hang this here. Who can say what thing, or person, belongs in a given place?

I pick up the news clipping again. A caption identifies the women and says, "The women were standing for a prayer that was given to end the day's session." Which means that the women stayed, even after the vote. I wouldn't have stayed, not to listen to a man pray in a venue that had just disallowed my voice.

I study the grainy photo again. The women's eyes are squeezed shut. Prayer as well as tears. I recognize their faithfulness. I'm impressed with their stamina. I'm touched by their silent doves and plucky yellow ribbons. They don't have to do this. They're not fighting for themselves, but for their daughters.

And here I am with my daughters. On this porch. Circling. Surrounded by growing corn. Feeding my daughters' fierce independence with the fodder of my mother's fight.

I pull Hannah and Clara onto my lap and smooth the hair back from their foreheads. I breathe deeply of the greeny air. I quote Dr. Seuss: "I meant what I said and I said what I meant. An elephant's faithful one hundred percent!"

The girls each nestle into a shoulder. Doug settles into the other chair and begins to read again. I smile as the eye-hooks creak rhythmically. I will let their complaint be our lullaby.

Couldn't You Wait
Until I'm Dead?

Rev. Patricia J. Raube

"Couldn't you wait until I'm dead?"

Thus spoke my mother (may she rest in peace) one fine spring afternoon. She and my father were visiting my suburban Boston home, and Dad was outside running my then two-and-a-half-year-old son Ned all around the yard. I was working on a master's degree in pastoral ministry—a program designed, in part, for the growing pool of lay men and women who sought the education and skills to serve in the Roman Catholic Church as vocations to the priesthood declined. I had just announced to my parents that I was considering leaving the church of my childhood because I felt a call to be ordained. (Dad had taken that as his cue to entertain Ned elsewhere).

Please understand. I loved my church. It was there that I learned who Jesus was and came to understand that his love for me was matched only by his love for other people—all other people, of every imaginable

Rev. Patricia J. Raube is pastor of Union Presbyterian Church in Endicott, New York. Prior to that she served in several interim positions, including that of interim chaplain of the Protestant Cooperative Ministry at Cornell University. She wrote "Blessed Is She Who Believes" for *Daughters of Sarah: The Magazine for Christian Feminists*. She blogs her sermons at upcsermonsandmore.blogspot.com and maintains an archive at ceciliainthecloset.blogspot.com. Her children, Ned and Joan, are finding their way as actors and artists, and her partner, Sher, continues to listen carefully, and always, always, speaks the truth in love.

description, and so I had better get on with the project of loving them as well. My church taught me that Jesus, who said odd things like "Blessed are the meek, for they will inherit the earth," had surprises in store for me.

But it was the very same church that first told me no when I sought to serve. When I was nine I wanted to be an altar girl—my brother had been an altar *boy*—and though I'd never heard of anyone else being an altar girl, I couldn't imagine what might prevent me from being one anyway.

My mother said nothing to discourage me. She made an appointment for us to see our parish priest, Monsignor O'Connor. She stood quietly by while I asked him, eagerly, "How do I become an altar girl?" And she listened with me to his kind and oddly encouraging negative reply: "*Right now*, girls cannot be altar servers," he said.

"But maybe later?" I asked. (At the age of nine, I knew well the dance of "Not now, maybe later.")

"Yes," he said, "I'm pretty sure it will happen, *but later.*"

For a long time, I was satisfied with that answer. After all, my church kept feeding me with the bread of life. But by the time I had reached my late twenties—I was twenty-nine when my mother asked me to await her death before making any sudden moves—I had come up hard against the limitations placed upon women in the church. I'd begun to hunger for a sermon from a woman's point of view. I'd subscribed to the Women's Ordination Conference newsletter. I'd spent the summer of my first pregnancy in crisis: Would I baptize this child in a church in which his own mother was unable to offer back to God the gifts she'd been given? I went on strike, attending not mass but Quaker meetings, belly growing, silent in the stifling air, wondering what on earth I would do.

In the end, it was the birth several years later, not of a son but of a daughter, that was the deciding factor. Joan (named for an extraordinary Benedictine nun with whom I'd studied, as well as my mother and the girl on fire) was born after I'd relocated to upstate New York and was attending an Episcopal church that I had not quite decided to join. One Sunday morning as I held Joan in the tiny children's chapel at the rear of the church, an excellent nursing space, the choir sang a rapturously beautiful rendition of "The King of Love My Shepherd Is." Joan lifted her head, turned toward the music, and began rooting in the air for the glorious sound. Something inside me cracked open. I recognized in my baby the same longing that was in me. We need beauty and connection as well as food—even a newborn knew that. But it required turning around—that biblical word *metanoia*, usually translated as "repentance." I needed to turn around and start moving toward that which would give me life.

"Couldn't you wait until I'm dead?"

Here's how I answered my mother: "Well, imagine that you were trying to do something you thought would make you happy, as well as answer God's call. And imagine your mother saying, 'Wait until I'm dead.' What would *you* say?"

Without missing a beat, she replied, "I'd tell her to go jump in the lake."

Please understand. I would never tell my mother to go jump in a lake. But in that moment, we understood one another. And we laughed, long and hard. And on the day of my ordination she celebrated with as much joy as anyone, as she saw her own daughter reaching out for beauty, for connection, for life.

The Accidental Leader

Rev. Robin Craig

It did not occur to me until about midway through seminary that the call to ministry is a call to leadership. My intention was to serve as a companion, a guide, a collaborator on the Christian journey. A fellow pilgrim. A sojourner who might help others encounter God as I had encountered God.

The concept of leadership was not directly addressed in seminary. We developed a bit of expertise in ancient languages and exegesis and homiletics, but those subjects primarily addressed communication skills. We studied pastoral care, but that one was about presence and counsel. We learned history and theology, but those courses were concerned with knowing and passing on the tradition. None of this sounded like leadership to me. And leadership was nowhere on my radar screen until one day a professor casually mentioned our future roles as leaders in the church. My ears perked up. Leaders? We were going to be *leaders*?

As for many pastors, my moment came. The first intimation that I had inadvertently answered a call to leadership occurred a couple of days after the forty-something administrative assistant at my small rural congregation died of a heart attack. As I sat with our council in an evening meeting,

---

Rev. Robin Craig is pastor of Boulevard Presbyterian Church in Euclid, Ohio, having previously served as pastor of Nankin Federated Church in Nankin, Ohio. She is also a spiritual director and retreat leader trained in the Ignatian tradition. Her article, "Ignatian Spirituality: Companionship in Loss," appeared in *Presence*, the journal of Spiritual Directors International. She blogs at metanoia-mrc. blogspot.com. Robin and her husband are the parents of three children, and are trying to figure out how to move gracefully into the third third of life.

I thought: *Someone needs to address what has happened. Someone needs to lead us in prayer and to offer some reassuring words.*

Oh, I suddenly realized. *That someone would be me!*

I became a member of a cohort of new pastors who directly addressed questions of leadership. We discussed the great biblical narratives of leadership, as well as topics like family systems and organizational behavior. We learned something about our own styles of leadership, and our own predilections for promoting—or resisting—change.

I was confused. I still had no plans to lead anyone anywhere. I had no leadership skills of which I was aware. I possessed no sense of intuition as far as leadership was concerned. I was, in short, a bit like Moses himself, whose response to God's call to leadership echoes through the millennia: "Who, me? Oh, please—find someone else!"

But maybe I had misunderstood. Maybe I had accidentally—or via the movement of the Holy Spirit, whose activities can look suspiciously accidental—discovered exactly what my calling was.

At first, I mostly understood what leadership is not. Leadership is not about administration—despite what our congregants may think. Leadership is not about care and companionship, it's not about teaching and preaching, and it's not about liturgical organization. All those matters are essential components of church leadership, but they can be done without much in the way of leadership skills.

So what is it, this elusive concept of leadership? What does it entail? And how do you learn it by accident?

I learned something about leadership by tumbling into the ongoing lives of those bound together by congregational ties, some of them solidly secured by three generations of church engagement and others awakened by a hospital visit. By discovering ways to elicit honest responses in difficult situations. By inviting folks into creative forms of worship and watching their delight and their dismay—sometimes on the same day. By looking around our community on a Sunday morning, noticing the missing pieces, and suggesting ways to fill the gaps. By teaching, both by words and by example, that asking questions is foundational to a life of discipleship. By pausing as people tell stories reflecting their deep longing for someone to help them articulate and shape their puzzling lives into coherent quests instigated by God, accompanied by Jesus, and fueled by the Spirit.

It turns out that leadership is founded upon attentiveness. By paying attention to the voices of my congregation, I learned what leadership is.

Leadership is about setting a tone, creating a vision, and negotiating priorities.

Leadership is about helping a congregation discover its own unfolding story.

Leadership is about challenging the church to live into the biblical narrative of a hope-filled journey.

Today I serve an inner-ring suburban church like so many others in the mainline denominations: Once thriving, now declining. Big building, small bank account. Many needs, little energy. My task is not to solve the problems, re-create the past, or transform the future. My role is to understand that God is doing a new thing, and to encourage my people to find the voice, the story, and the vision into which God is inviting them.

It is now my delight to say to a struggling band of fellow pilgrims, "Come and see." My delight, and the words of Jesus. That would be leadership. Perhaps not accidental at all.

Worn In

Rev. Dr. Teri McDowell Ott

"Is your daddy a pastor?" The carpet salesman cocked his head after I inquired about the clergy discount I'd heard he offered. Stepping back from his question, I averted my eyes. I was fresh out of seminary, newly ordained as an associate pastor at a church in South Carolina. I wasn't from the South. Was this a Southern thing? Are all pastors men here? And my father's age?

"No." I answered. "I'm the pastor."

His yellow button-down shirt was wet below the armpits and tucked into wrinkled khaki pants. I guessed we were about the same age—late twenties. But, by the look on his face, we were worlds apart. He couldn't hide his surprise.

Standing there in the clothes I'd been unloading boxes in all day (an old T-shirt, jean shorts, and Birkenstocks), I contemplated this man's assumptions. Suddenly, I realized something I had yet to consider. I didn't look like a minister.

Rev. Dr. Teri McDowell Ott has been an ordained Presbyterian minister for over fifteen years. After receiving her master of divinity degree from Louisville Presbyterian Theological Seminary, she served the church in a variety of positions and serves Monmouth College in Monmouth, Illinois, as chaplain. Teri blogs regularly at Something to Say (somethingtosayblog.com) and recently published an article in the *Christian Century* titled "Wilderness Venture: Toward a More Honest Sermon." Teri and her husband, Dan, have two towheaded, energetic young children, Isaac and Ella, whom they enjoy immensely, and one skittish German shepherd mix named Percy.

This became more of a problem when I began dealing with funeral directors on a regular basis. These older Southern men never called on me as an authority. When decisions needed to be made about closed or open caskets, or whether Great-Grandma Flossie's portrait could be displayed on the communion table, they deferred to the other pastors in my church or the parishioners. I also grew increasingly irritable every time they referred to me as "precious," "dearie," or "honey," oftentimes accompanied by a little pat on the back.

I needed to make a change. So I spoke to my hairdresser about dyeing my blond highlighted hair black and I shopped for a pair of serious-looking glasses. Then I remembered the time my senior pastor and I dressed up for Reformation Sunday, ordering ourselves clerical collars with Geneva tabs. Neither of us had any experience with these collars—it's not the norm to wear them in the Presbyterian Church. And I never did figure out how to fasten the two-fingered piece of white cloth onto the plastic tab collar. On that Reformation Sunday I secured it with Scotch Tape, hoping no one would notice.

Wearing the collar stayed with me, though. I remembered the attention and authority it brought. So I started shopping for the clerical collar that I decided would accompany me to every funeral.

There weren't many styles or colors to choose from—tab or round collar, black or gray shirt in a cotton-polyester blend. I ordered over the phone after measuring my neck. The catalog told me I needed a size 10–12. Typically, I wear a size 6. When I received the shirt and tried it on, it fit like a big black garbage bag cinched at the neck.

The first time I saw myself in the mirror, I flushed in embarrassment. Checking my reflection from all sides—front, back, left profile, right—I panicked at the idea of wearing the collar for real, not just for dress-up on Reformation Sunday. *This isn't me*, I thought to myself. *I can't wear this thing.*

Staring at this stranger, foreign in her clerical authority, I realized that the collar wasn't just for the old, male funeral directors, or those who mistook me for the church secretary. It was also for *me*. This collar had work to do.

There was no denying the power of the piece of plastic at my throat when I wore it to my first funeral. Suddenly, I was the one in charge—greeted by the funeral director with a polite "ma'am." The collar quickly set me apart in a way that felt right and respectful. It created a distance between the people and me that I sensed was appreciated, as if those gathered knew they were in good hands. Also, for the first time in my ministry, I felt myself embody the role of preacher and pastor. The collar gave me gravitas. It helped me stand up a little straighter. It coaxed holy liturgy from my throat.

Times have changed in the world of clergy apparel. After what seems like a brief fifteen years of ministry, I can now buy a clerical collar dress (A-line or drop waist) or shirt made of flattering stretchy fabric. Tempted to be trendier, I've considered retiring my black garbage bag. But then I put my shirt on, button it to my neck, and tuck the white plastic tab into its fabric folds. This preworship ritual feels like I am suiting up for battle, as much as I hate the militaristic metaphor. It's not a battle against outside forces though, but against the forces within—my own fear and insecurity. As I suit up, I notice that the black is fading to gray and the collar's edge has begun to fray. I could order a new shirt. But the old one speaks to me of a woman who has worn herself into her calling—and of a God who always urges me to be more than I could ever imagine for myself.

I Sit at My Desk
A Prayer

Rev. Julia Seymour

God of all space and time,

As I approach your people,
I feel the shade of Deborah's palm over me,
The heft of Elijah's staff in my hand,
The pleas of David on my lips,
The resistance of the prophets in my feet,
The confusion of the disciples at the forefront of mind.

I sit at my desk and wait for your Spirit
To inspire my writing,
To keep me from slamming down the phone,
To help me listen to the same story over and over,
To breathe life into the coals of my joy,
To celebrate with me in moments of pleasure.

I live out this curious vocation.
Serving your people goes with my tasks as a

Rev. Julia Seymour has been the ordained minister at Lutheran Church of Hope in Anchorage, Alaska, since August 2008. She believes strongly in ecumenical and interfaith cooperation. She blogs at lutheranjulia.blogspot.com. Julia enjoys reading, writing, crochet, and outdoor activities. She lives with her husband, their two young children, and their devoted Labrador retriever.

Child, parent, sibling, friend, partner,
Lover, neighbor, cousin, grandchild,
Customer, passerby, fellow traveler, pot stirrer.

There are always more identities,
held under the pastoral mantle, with their own work.
Tears of highest joy and deepest grief to dry.
There are goings and comings, celebrations of all kinds.
There are lists, plans, prayers, homilies,
Half-baked plans and hopes that burst forth from the fruits
    of the Spirit
And some that wither on the vine.
And somehow, in all of this,

Christ comes.

I confess that I am not always aware of him,
Even as I'm seeking him.

But then, I turn, I see his calling card.

The healing. The grace. The hope.
And so ministry continues—
Even in me.

Thanks be to you.

Finding My Voice

Rev. Hilary Campbell

"It's wonderful to see how you have blossomed over the past few years. You really seem to have found your voice." It was at a summer school during my time of training for ordained ministry that I heard this. The words came as a surprise, as compliments often do for me, but they warmed my heart, and I knew that they were true—I *had* found my voice; I was finding the way and the words to speak out in faith.

I've never been an adventurous soul. Maybe that's why, early in my life, I discovered a love of stories. Stories that I could hide in, reinvent myself in, do some vicarious adventuring through. Along the way of discovering my own voice, one of the things I have found to be important is the whole process of searching for words, reaching out for them, then trying out how they fit and make meaning for me.

When it comes to finding a way of belonging in the world, including the world of the church, I guess I've always looked for the narrative that brings together the human experience of life and faith. Questions and doubting, metaphors and ideas pushed the boundaries and opened the possibilities of faith for me.

Stories set me on my way, but it's been people who have helped me continue this human exploring and crafting, helped me bring faith down

---

Rev. Hilary Campbell is currently vicar for the Shires' Edge Benefice (a group of five rural parishes in North Oxfordshire, England). She was formerly team vicar in the parish of Kidlington with Hampton Poyle (just north of Oxford, England). She blogs at Pootling Along (revhillersblog.wordpress.com). Hilary is a ukulele-playing, singing storyteller and an Anglican vicar.

to earth. The vicar at my home church showed me an unostentatious, committed, and unselfish way of living out the Christian faith that maybe one day I'll get close to copying. And becoming a mother was a life-altering experience that once again shook up the story I had about myself.

Now I find myself in the role of an ordained minister in the Church of England. What does this mean for the story of who I am and the work I do?

Sometimes it means facing conflict and challenge: "I've been contacted by two members of the congregation who are concerned you may have lost your faith. I need you to come to a meeting with them about this," said my colleague, after I preached on the creed. "I thought vicars were meant to comfort, not to cause more pain," in response to some pastoral reconciliation I was attempting.

Sometimes it means connection, as people say, "I'm so glad you said that about the creed—I thought I was the only one who couldn't believe." There are many folks wondering if their words and story fit with that presented by the church.

"What is your approach to preaching?" I was once asked at a preinterview "social" occasion. "It's like walking a tightrope," I replied. I meant that I often tried (and still do) to find a balance, to take care to offer words that many can catch and question and hold on to for a while. I'm still learning how to embrace this metaphor and enjoy the risk of adventure, the risk of alienating, the risk of vulnerable wobbling, the risk of daring to use my own voice.

One way I have found liberation is in learning the craft of storytelling. I've learned it firsthand from the women delightedly sharing Bible stories with the preschool group, and from sharing stories in school assemblies. Then I realized that it's not only children who need stories. My experience of telling and retelling stories from the Christian tradition is that they invariably lead to good questions and conversations: "Is it all right to think or say this?" Truth always goes about the world clothed in story—as an old story tells us. The power of storytelling includes the wonderful way that trusting the story, being faithful to story, can also involve creating something new for teller and listener. I'm slowly learning that the risk of setting aside the written words can be part of the process of finding a voice for myself in a leadership role and finding a voice for a community.

As a priest, I work to find words, story, and language to lay alongside the life experiences of the people I am with, to enable those stories to be heard and told. I hope that people will find for themselves a way into a story where they belong and can become their truest selves. As for me—it also helps when I'm surprised by being heard, by being called by name, like Mary in the garden.

> Good news, she said.
> Walking in the garden
> with the blush of spring sunshine,
> soft grass beneath her feet.
>
> Walking in the garden,
> memories all around,
> soft grass beneath her feet,
> ahead the sound of her name.
>
> Memories all around,
> with the blush of spring sunshine,
> ahead the sound of her name.
> Good news, she said.[*]

* A Pantoum Poem © 2013 by Hilary Campbell

High Heels in the Pulpit

Rev. Rachel G. Hackenberg

When I began seminary, a wise mentor told me, "Never wear jeans."

I understood. I was entering a prestigious theological school with an Ivy League name, the kind of academic environment where master's students with PhD aspirations treated the suit-and-bowtie ensemble as a prerequisite for their doctoral studies. Those of us pursuing the master's degree in preparation for pastoral ministries were no less ambitious than the PhD-destined; we unequivocally chose a theological school whose name would make an impression on paper and positively impact our career trajectories. With a few dressed-down exceptions, the student body took seriously that we were training to be church professionals— the parish-bound and the PhD-bound alike—and our attire reflected that goal.

It wasn't only the academic environment that discouraged anything less than business casual. Taking my attire seriously as a female seminarian on campus conveyed the message that I expected to be taken seriously as a female minister in church. Of course, a woman's outfit cannot compel anyone to take her seriously, and a number of male seminarians and ministers insisted (and still insist!) upon proving their disparagement of

Rev. Rachel G. Hackenberg is an author, United Church of Christ minister, and soccer mom. Her books include *Sacred Pause: A Creative Retreat for the Word-Weary Christian* and she blogs at faithandwater.com. Rachel currently serves on the national staff of the United Church of Christ. This story is not a critique of her clergy sisters' style choices, only a reflection on her own ... including the fabulous high heels she is determined to wear until her knees need replacement.

female colleagues. No matter a woman's professional attire, academic prowess, ministerial skills, or theological perspective, some men cannot see beyond a patriarchal interpretation of church and scripture and body. Some women, too, adopt this patriarchal lens for their own worldview. For such narrow-minded folks, a woman's gender negates her skills, her call, and fundamentally her equal personhood.

To be clear, however, I wasn't dressing to impress the naysayers at seminary or to prove my place as a serious theological student. I dressed to express the sincerity with which I was responding to God's call and with which I was preparing for ministry, and I continue to utilize clothing to communicate respect for and competence in this vocation.

Since entering ordained ministry, my professional wardrobe has taken on a necessarily conservative tone. A woman pastor simply cannot sit at a bedside in a hospital room fearing busty exposure by a loose blouse if she leans forward to hold a hand in prayer. She can't meet the senior church women's group for tea in a miniskirt that echoes the rebellion of these women's daughters. She daren't officiate a wedding in denim or preside over communion in her favorite sweats. Much of this is a no-brainer (I hope and pray). Ministry requires a certain decorum of attire—for both women and men—and my closet reflects this practical conservatism in browns and blacks and grays.

I like the simplicity of a professional wardrobe, truth be told. It's the casual events of life that perplex my fashion sensibilities: my children's soccer games, the occasional town parade, an afternoon at the museum. How on earth do women dress for these occasions?

In a pantsuit, I feel every bit a woman and a minister, fully authentic and capable. A neutral professional wardrobe also suits my theology of the ministry: the minister is called to be a visible priestly authority and pastoral presence, who simultaneously is transparent (not invisible) in such a way that God's presence and work have the ultimate visibility. The minister is called to be fully enfleshed in her own particularities and to bear the sacred particularities of God within the world, to function fully as herself and as a reflection of God.

A conservative professional wardrobe conveys my theology of ministry and my sense of self ... especially when partnered with a stunning pair of heels to give a fashion nod to the divinely surprising and exuberantly audacious God! The seriousness of a professional wardrobe should not be misunderstood as being personally dull or theologically stern. Fashionable heels, I've concluded, express the joy of incarnational ministry without compromising the practical need for conservative attire.

So this is how I minister: In four-inch red heels. In chunky black heels with silky bows. In bright pink pumps and zebra-striped flats and even lush purple snow boots. Just a hint of personality with the professional image, a brightly confident accessory that says, *This woman, in these shoes, is a particular embodiment of God's ministry in the world.*

This woman, equipped to pronounce the good news of resurrection, in these high heels.

High heels to whisper the mystery of incarnation.

High heels to bury and high heels to marry.

High heels to preach and high heels to teach.

High heels for a seriously fabulous calling.

Queer

Rev. Katie Mulligan

i have been so reluctant to write this piece.
what does it mean to be
queer
in ministry?
last week (was it just?)
a church wrote to me. they wrote to me
as a colleague (Dear Brother or Sister in Christ or some such)
eleven pages to say—no, to *prove*—that they were dying
because of the gay
so they want to leave. to go away. to take their football.
they want a divorce, and they want to take the house with
    them.
they are sure i understand, or at least that i could if only
if only i could put myself in their shoes
(their ugly shoes).

Rev. Katie Mulligan currently is a youth and young adult pastor for three churches in and around Trenton, New Jersey (Ewing, Lawrence Road, and Covenant Presbyterian Churches), and a chaplain at Rider University. Formerly she served as pastor at New Covenant Presbyterian Church in Mount Laurel, New Jersey. She is the author of "A Ministry of Discomfort" in *From Each Brave Eye: Reflections on the Arts, Ministry, and Holy Imagination*. Her writing on LGBTQ concerns, intimate violence, and theology can be found at insideouted.blogspot. com and she is otherwise known as @grammercie on Twitter. She is a graduate of Princeton Theological Seminary and ordained as a teaching elder in the Presbyterian Church. She is the mother of two sons. Also, cats. The reverend adores cats.

What would it be like for me if I had to exist in a hostile
    environment? For however many long years, had to sit by
    and watch while my marriage rights/rites were stripped of
    their meaning?
yeah. what would that be?
i think they should install me as pastor there
to give wings to their feet.
two-thirds would be gone in a week.

a few years ago a colleague and i shared breakfast.
he made me an astounding offer.
judge, dear reader, why don't you?
"The godly thing to do" (he said while chewing oatmeal)
"would be to renounce your ordination.
I know you have children. You could come live with us."
"Have you spoken to your wife about this?"
"No," he said, "but she is a godly woman."
(long pause)
"Well," I said, "my ex-husband would be coming with us.
He will need his own room."
(furrowed eyebrows)
"Also, I have four cats. And some fish. Do you think my
    china hutch will fit in your dining room? I don't want
    to impose, but my grandmother gave me those dishes
    for my wedding and promptly died. I'm partial to
    keeping them."
(crickets chirping)
"Can you pass the salt? These eggs are bland. Oh, this is
    going to be great. I have always wanted a sister-wife."
(frowny face)
"You are not taking me seriously," he said.
"No kidding."

what is it to be queer in ministry?
what is it to be queer?
or in ministry?
how can you stand to be straight?

how has ministry not sent you shrieking
with rage
and grief
into the sweet balm of
queer love
queer thinking
our so very queer Lord and Savior?

a straight man
a very angry straight man (a very straight angry man?)
someone i have not met (and hope to never)
sent me this sweet epistle
(i think he thought he was Paul—and how queer was *that*
    guy?)
The subject line read *Anathama.*

You are a disgrace to the faith. You are an unrepentant
    sinner in the eyes of God and He does not forgive
    the unrepentant. If you are a Presbyterian leave
    the denomination and take your lack of obedience
    somewhere else. It is queers like you who have
    denigrated this denomination and have said: "I will
    rather have half of a dead baby than none of a live and
    healthy one."
You personally are a disgrace. And you and your ilk have
    caused me to be ashamed of my denomination.
With no respect for you,
xxxxxxxxxxxxxxxxxxx
Retired PC (USA)

Dear Brother in Christ, you misspelled *anathema*
but Jesus covers even this.

what is it to be queer in ministry?
it is to be the angel of death,
the harbinger of disease and pestilence.
(did you not know we can kill you dead from AIDS just by
    looking at you?)

i am the despoiler of churches i have never set foot in
the destruction of marriages i would never have officiated.
i am come, like Lilith,
to feast on your children.
i am not subordinate
a winged demon in the night
the opposite of Eve.
my cooking pot is straight out of Proverbs 666.
if i were you
(and oh so glad i am not)
i would not eat the food i serve you.
more. for. me.
wipe the dust
for i will not hear your gospel.
i am called to dance by one who delights in me.
take back your peace
for there is clearly none to be had here.
i don't actually care about your
building, your
marriage, your
childr—
No.
that is not true
i care about your children
and by extension your marriage
and by extension your damned building.

what is it to be queer in ministry?
it is to be spat upon
and still give a rat's ass
about the person who spat
in my face.
a very queer thing indeed.

Leaving Well

Rev. Amy Fetterman

God and I had a deal. I would go to seminary and God, in turn, would call me to a church in a fabulously fun big city. I kept up my part of the bargain; God, not so much. Rather than bring me to an exciting metropolis, God decided to call me to be the associate pastor for a church in a town with no mass transit, no Target, and no Thai food! I answered this call, but wondered if maybe God had gotten something wrong.

It turns out *I* was wrong. I fell in love with the church, the people, and the town. I made amazing friends and met my spouse here. I grew in my ministry and identity as a pastor. I participated in God's kingdom in exciting ways I hadn't even dreamt of when I left seminary. I loved this call.

Cue that meddlesome God. I loved the people I served, loved the ministry we had done together, and yet eight years in I began to get this nagging sense that an end was nearing. I saw affirmation of my ministry in the self-sufficient programs, in the strong lay leadership, in the life-bringing cultural shift that developed during my time at the church. I also saw affirmation that I had indeed accomplished what God had called me to do here. It was time to go.

Rev. Amy Fetterman is currently trying her hand at being a full-time stay-at-home parent and part-time doctoral student. She previously served as associate pastor at Covenant Presbyterian Church in Staunton, Virginia. She is coauthor of *Who's Got Time? Spirituality for a Busy Generation* and blogs at the book's website, spiritualityforbusypeople.com. She loves traveling, napping, cooking, and geeking out over Joss Whedon, Harry Potter, and the BBC.

Once I accepted God's new call, the question shifted from *if* I should leave to *how* I should leave. The general model in my denomination calls for giving around four to six weeks' notice, during which the church recovers from its surprise, says good-bye, and perhaps begins to grieve. The pastor scrambles to make sure everything is covered until an interim comes, preaches the farewell sermon, and hits the road. This model works well enough, yet my own circumstances offered an opportunity for something different.

I knew God was calling me to something new, I just didn't know what that new thing would be. My options were limited, as I was tethered to a specific geographic area by my spouse's job—a job that could financially support both of us. With this financial support, I didn't need to have a new job lined up in order to answer the call to leave. After prayer and conversations with my spouse and colleagues, I shared with my church that I would be leaving after the end of the program year—six months from my announcement.

Six months instead of six weeks is a bit odd—and what a wonderfully blessed oddity. The congregation and I got to process this change, celebrate our shared ministry, start a transition, and say good-bye without any rush. Those six months also gave me time to think about what unique things I had brought to the church that would be missed when I left. Primarily I thought about the young women who had grown up with me as one of their pastors, who had a built-in role model, who were developing their own identity as women of faith.

I did not want to leave these young women without a role model. As I looked around the church, I realized I didn't have to. Strong, smart women of faith filled the pews of the church—they just didn't naturally leave those pews to reach out to the younger generation. One of the downsides of having a thriving, distinct youth group is that the youth of the church become an unintentionally segregated population. The young women of my church interacted with people their own age, plus the handful of adult leaders who felt called to that ministry. They missed out on being in relationship with members of all ages—members who could be role models after I left.

I invited women across the generations—from the ninth grade to the ninth decade—to join together for fellowship and service once a month for four months. We engaged with biblical stories of women's relation-ships and shared our own experiences of being women. The older gen-eration marveled at the minds and character of the younger women; the younger women delighted in the connections they made with the older women and the encouragement they felt through these relationships. By the end of this intentional time, I knew I would be leaving these younger women with plenty of role models.

Whether or not I ever leave another call with as much notice as I did this one, I hope this experience of leaving well seeps into other transition experiences I may have. I hope I will be aware of those meaningful aspects of my ministry that haven't yet been integrated into the congregation's life and will be missed when I go, so that when I first feel those stirrings of the Spirit, I can think about how to offer a legacy to the church. Once I'm gone, a church may miss me, but I hope they will not miss the unique gifts I brought.

Balls

Rev. Kathryn Z. Johnston

Confident.
Assertive.
Powerful.

"She packs her penis in her purse."

When I first heard one of my male colleagues describe a female colleague this way, I was admittedly taken aback.

Don't get me wrong, I'm from New Jersey, along the same route that's shown in the opening of the *Sopranos*—and I've heard some colorful language in my day. But this charming colloquialism had somehow escaped me.

Strong.
Straight-talking.
Decisive.

She packs her penis in her purse? What the hell is that supposed to mean?

Rev. Kathryn Z. Johnston is senior pastor and head of staff at Mechanicsburg Presbyterian Church in Mechanicsburg, Pennsylvania. She previously served as solo pastor at Dickinson Presbyterian Church in Carlisle, Pennsylvania, as well as in youth ministry positions in churches in Florida before seminary. Her blog is Volume II (kathrynzj.blogspot.com). Kathryn's home life includes the editor of *There's a Woman in the Pulpit*, Rev. Martha Spong, hers and hers children (four total), two cats, and a garage full of balls (soccer, baseball, football, volleyball ... even croquet).

The conversation was about an older colleague who had gone to serve at one of our denomination's flagship churches, and the rumors were flying about her tumultuous relationship with a congregation that had never had a female senior pastor before.

I heard descriptions of her crimes against humanity. (Hu*man*ity, that is.) Most of her moves seemed reasonable, with the only major flaw being timing. Some ministers have an unwritten rule that when you arrive at a church you change nothing for a year. She took the opposite approach. When men do this, it is described as "Trying to move too quickly" or "Getting ahead of the congregation" or "He didn't let them know he loved them first."

Her? Well, clearly she is worthy of a Lorena Bobbitt flashback, accessorized by Vera Bradley.

> Self-reliant.
> In-charge.
> Leader.

It's a fact of the female pastor's life: if we act in a way that would get men heralded as leaders, we are instead labeled as bitches. I have had conversations with both women and men, in which I could tell that if I had a balding head, a collared shirt and tie—and, oh yes ... a penis—then the idea I was conveying would be considered "genius" rather than prompting the thought, *She has some nerve.*

As I've gotten older and more experienced, I've learned to choose my battles. There are times when I need support for an idea from the guys on Team Penis, but I also know I won't get it if the idea comes from me. Rather than doing battle alone from my self-righteous feminist foundation, I recruit men who respect women in leadership to rally for the cause and help me bridge the gap between me—woman with ovaries—and them—Neanderthals with dragging knuckles.

> Independent.
> Honorable.
> Authoritative.

On the Enneagram I am an 8. I have sprinkled the words that are used to describe 8s throughout this story. I also googled *describe a man*. A lot of the same words showed up. Also included were: *high performance, direct,* and *resilient*. I then googled *describe a woman*. What I got was: *bossy, clingy,* and *cold*.

I then googled *packs her penis in her purse*.

Don't do that.

Actually, I did do that and then clicked on *images*, prepared to turn quickly away. There were none of the pictures that you might think (whew!) and interestingly enough the first two recognizable women in the picture gallery were Hillary Clinton and Michelle Obama. (There was also Rihanna, inexplicably carrying a penis purse, but that's for another story.)

> Courageous.
> Protective.
> Commanding.

I am a leader.

If people do not like the decisions I make or the way I lead, that is a conflict they have with my personality, not my gender. The lack of a Y chromosome has nothing to do with anything and shouldn't impact the way people interact with me.

Except for this ...

After a long term of service to the church, marked by petulant, passive-aggressive, and bullying maneuvers, a staff member turned her sights on me. Her last line of defense was a threatened resignation. The technique had worked with countless male pastors before me—she'd threaten to resign, and then came the concessions. The staff member was allowed to do whatever she wanted.

After months of attempting to get on the same page but holding my ground, the threatened resignation came. The difference was, I accepted.

Now, petulant, passive-aggressive, bullying types don't stay around for decades by accident. This staff member had plenty of friends and connections in the congregation, and her final Sunday was not an enjoyable one for me. I absorbed my fair share of glares and stood silently as mistruths were spoken in hushed tones only a few feet away from me.

Finally, an older gentleman, who had quite some tenure in the church and was known for his gentle wisdom, sidled up to me and shook my hand. "I need to tell you something. That staff member has been wreaking havoc here for decades and has never been called on it. It's about time someone had the balls to do it."

I looked at him and said, "Thank you."

And I don't even own a purse.

Come Down and Help, Please

Rev. Sally-Lodge Teel

There are many things I don't like to remember about Hurricane Katrina: pines down, massive oaks stripped of branches, homes washed away or broken by falling trees, landmarks erased from familiar places. The physical changes to our everyday view of this place were horrific. Years later, rebuilding goes on, but every day I drive the beach road I see huge empty spaces still. The world changed on August 29, 2005.

My world changed in ways I could not imagine. My home was surrounded by fallen trees, my husband's law office disappeared, pushed back into a wall of several-story-high debris, and the wind twisted the sanctuary of my church. Katrina damaged not just the world around me, so that I could not find my way around a once-known place, but it damaged, too, the people around me.

Standing in line at the temporary post office that looked more like an ice cream truck than an official building, people talked about what they

---

Rev. Sally-Lodge Teel, a Presbyterian Church (USA) minister and a graduate of Columbia Theological Seminary, lives in Mississippi with her husband; they have two grown children. In 1978, she was the first Presbyterian woman ordained in the state of Mississippi. It would be no exaggeration to name Sally-Lodge as the founder of RevGalBlogPals, for she posed the foundational question "Should we have a T-shirt?" at her blog, stcasseroleblog.blogspot.com. She loves her small church in Pearl River County, where the congregants still teach her about faith and ministry.

had lost: homes, cars, jobs, photos. Going to the grocery store, people gathered to comfort each other, grab purified water, and cry. The Walmart parking lot on Highway 49, a huge expanse of asphalt, became town center, where people went to find help and to socialize. People were traumatized, sick with worry, and stir-crazy, with nowhere to go and nothing to do but try to organize the debris around their homes.

Katrina damaged me too. The howling winds and rising water blew into my life and took away my confidence in federal and state help, and showed me suffering I wept to see. It made me feel helpless and hopeless to do ministry. Sure, I could house volunteers who came to help my neighbors. I could help clean up the debris piles. I could listen to the stories of grief everyone spewed out as they tried to make sense of their situations. But my interior life was shattered. I stopped sleeping and eating; I stared out windows, looking for something I could not find. When I prayed, I was overwhelmed. When I returned to weekly preaching, I stood in the pulpit and fought the urge to weep instead of speak.

Several months before Katrina, I had started looking around the Internet for other clergywomen. I am in a small presbytery (a geographic cluster of Presbyterian churches) and I was one of three women preachers. The other two lived hours away from me. I was lonely. Through searching the web, I found women one by one who were doing the work of ministry, and we became friends. I read their blogs, and they read mine. One night, in a burst of happiness, I suggested we design a T-shirt for ourselves. The blog comment thread became hilarious, with suggestions from clergywomen around the States about what the T-shirt might say. Thus began RevGalBlogPals.

I had no clue that these RevGals would be agents of God's movement in my life. I was just glad to have friends to talk with about ministry, our families, and all the curious things about being a clergywoman.

Hearing about the hurricane, the RevGals reached out to me online. I don't think we had phone numbers or even real names for each other back then. They knew me only by a blogging nickname, St. Casserole. When asked what I needed, I put out the call for help for pastors on the Gulf Coast who were having a terrible time coping with the storm aftermath. We didn't need sweaters or old tennis shoes; we needed respite for exhausted preachers and pastoral care for our congregations. One of the

RevGals volunteered to fly down in January to preach for me and for a United Methodist clergywoman, and to do what she could to help with pastoral care. I grabbed at her offer. I did not know her, nor she me, but come down and help, please.

I wore my RevGalBlogPals T-shirt to pick her up at the Gulfport-Biloxi airport, knowing she would not recognize me. She came from Portland. I'll admit here what I've never admitted to her: I was so damaged I didn't know if she was flying in from Portland, Maine, or Portland, Oregon. Just come and help. Be with me through this agony and confusion. Help me remember who I am when I can't cope. Help me help.

She came from Maine. She preached for my Methodist friend and then gave toys to the congregation's children. She brought a cherished possession for me: a prayer shawl from her congregation's prayer shawl ministry. She sat with me, talked with me, and went around my community, offering love and help. She cooked for my family, beginning a tradition we cherish to this day—the Festival of Meat Loaf.

Healing came because she came.

A Taste of Heaven
and a Splash of Glory

Sharing the Sacraments

Do this in remembrance of me.

LUKE 22:19

They are the visible signs of invisible grace. They are reminders, cues, and tangible symbols of mysteries we can scarcely comprehend, even on our best days. They are miracles enacted with humble, ordinary elements: juice or wine from a modern bottle that has been plucked from a store shelf; bread either purchased or home-baked in an oven that could be found in any of millions of kitchens; water from the tap. Yet, through the mechanism of grace, they are transformed.

They are the sacraments.

We share these stories from the font, be it a simple bowl, a cherished church treasure, or perhaps the edge of a river. We share these stories from the table: graceful and white-clothed, worn and water-ringed, a humble picnic table or at the hospital bedside. As we share them, we offer a glimpse into the vulnerability we feel when we dare to pronounce a child of God welcomed into the fold "in the name of the Father, and of the Son, and of the Holy Spirit," or when handing a mouthful of bread and a sip of wine to an octogenarian and offering it up as the body and blood of Christ himself. Such audacious claims we mere mortals make!

But mostly, we offer what *we* have found in these acts: a taste of heaven and a splash of glory.

Drop by Precious Drop

Suzy Garrison Meyer

I always peek. "Bless these, your gifts," I pray, and I always look down to make sure my hand is hovering safely and is in no danger of sending the pitcher flying. On some Sundays, we could have laughed about something like that, but we'd just lost a woman dear to us all. Our hearts were hurting.

Most of the saints of our church die elsewhere. Winters in the Rocky Mountains are too long and too hard for our older members, so they leave in October, after they've seen the aspens flame one more time. And in the dark days of January and February, the phone calls come.

The rituals that might comfort us usually are conducted far away. All winter, the frozen ground of our cemetery lies under several feet of snow, so the funerals mostly take place elsewhere, in the communities where children and grandchildren have moved because our town has few jobs. Maybe in the summer there'll be a memorial service, a scattering of ashes, but usually it's just us, the faithful remnant now reduced by one, huddled in the chilly sanctuary on the first Sunday morning after sad news.

On those mornings, it seems especially poignant to share communion with the faithful of every time and place, in a church where we've shared communion so often with those who've gone before.

Suzy Garrison Meyer is a commissioned ruling elder in the Presbyterian Church (USA) and the tent-making pastor of a small but tenacious church in the mountains of Colorado. Retired from a long career as a newspaper publisher, she currently works in public relations to support her book habit. She and her husband, Marc, who have two grown children, are now chipping away at their bucket lists.

Ours is an old church for this part of the country, built in 1892, and lacking indoor plumbing until 2002—yes, the twenty-first century. It's an austere, barnlike building, with a soaring ceiling and thin, clear glass in its windows, because the beauty of God's creation here outshines any stained-glass artistry. The stove warms the air, at least to a point at which we can no longer see our breath, but throughout the winter the building's bones remain chilled.

The communion table is reputed to be the only one ever used there. It's a dainty piece of Eastlake furniture, and its marble top, cool to the touch even in July and August, has survived more than 120 years without a chip. On communion Sundays, we cover the bread with a good linen napkin while we hold choir practice and Sunday school. That way nobody's bustling in with bread and juice at the last moment. There's no danger of forgetting.

The system had never failed us, until that Sunday in February when I slowly understood that I was peeking down at a lovely, crusty loaf—and purple ice. Not just a delicate tracing of crystals across the surface of the blood of Christ I was preparing to pour out for us all, but a solid disk of frozen juice.

In panic, I risked a glance at my husband in the front pew. For once, his head was properly bowed. Still saying the prayer, I picked up the pitcher and wiggled it gently. The ice didn't budge. I tipped it over the chalice. Nothing dribbled out. I thought, almost hysterically, that I had found the one challenge that Christ never had to confront. On a day when the promise of the resurrection was so important for my congregation to hear, I held the Popsicle of salvation.

The prayer had to end, and when I raised my head and looked out at the faces gazing back at me, I realized that I could trust the body of Christ in this place. I didn't have to solve the problem of the frozen juice; I could let it be. How many times have I had to learn that I'm not in control?

Words came—words about loss and enduring love, about how many memories live on in our sanctuary and in our collective understanding of the bread and the juice. All the while, I cradled the pitcher close, and I walked, first as close to the stove as I dared and then to the opposite side of the sanctuary and back.

Then I pronounced the words of institution and raised the pitcher and the cup so that the whole congregation could see whatever was going to happen.

Thanks be to God, the juice poured. Not all of it—chunks of ice came too, splashing dark droplets on the white linen.

The blood of Christ, poured out for the many.

Of Water and the Body

Rev. Joanna Harader

I heard about a conversation between two pastors—a sprinkler and a dunker.

The sprinkler says, "So do people have to go all the way under the water for the baptism to count?"

The dunker says, "Yes. Absolutely."

"What if they go under just up to their chin?"

"Doesn't count."

"What if they go all the way up to their eyeballs? Or *almost* all the way under?"

"Still doesn't count."

"So," says the sprinkler to the dunker, "I was right all along. It's the top of the head that really matters."

While I would not go so far as to say that sprinkling doesn't count, I will admit to a deep prejudice toward dunking. I don't know if it is because of my symbolism-loving soul or my Baptist roots, but I love immersion. I love it for the physical reenactment of burial and resurrection; for the sense of being fully enveloped by the holy; for the suggestion of complete and gleaming cleanness.

Rev. Joanna Harader serves as pastor of Peace Mennonite Church in Lawrence, Kansas. She lives with her mother (Rev. Cheryl Harader, also a contributor to *There's a Woman in the Pulpit*), husband, three children, two dogs, two cats, two cockatiels, five chickens, and a hamster. And yes, sometimes she has to hide in her bedroom to get any writing done.

As a pastor, though, I have realized that, while the *symbolism* of immersion is practically perfect in every way, the *practicality* of immersion leaves a lot to be desired.

To begin with, getting a big tub of water into the sanctuary is not easy, if you don't already have one built in behind the curtains at the front. We actually moved a stock tank into our sanctuary once. It took forever to fill—partly because (since I was getting in that thing too) the water had to be heated. Which meant boiling pots of water on the stove and dumping them into the tank along with the water coming out of the hose we had pulled in through the window.

And then the physical act of dunking. Did I mention that I'm five feet tall? In a tradition where people are generally sixteen or older when they're baptized, this means that everyone I have ever baptized has been taller than me. Which is OK. My worship professor, who is over six feet tall, made me dunk him during our baptism practice session, so I knew I could do it. Still, climbing into a stock tank and getting someone a head taller than me all the way under the surface of the water is somewhat physically awkward.

I continue to love the symbolism of immersion. If I ever write a book or poem about baptism, you can bet there will be redeemed bodies rising from the water, diamond droplets dripping from their wet, holy heads.

But when it comes to the physical, practical realities of officiating a baptism in a building with no big bathtub, I have come to appreciate the more common practice of my particular Mennonite tradition: pouring. Those being baptized kneel in front of the congregation and I simply pour water from a pitcher over their heads.

Granted, I use a lot of water when I pour—much to the dismay of one poor man who ended up last in the baptismal line. I poured all the (cold) water left in the pitcher over his head. "Am I a worse sinner than everyone else that you had to use so much extra water on me?" he wanted to know.

I assured him that the amount of water used makes no difference when it comes to the ultimate effect of the baptism. And that is true in more ways than one. Immersion counts. Pouring counts. I suppose, in a drought, sprinkling would suffice.

This reality relieves me and scares me all at the same time. Because if baptism were ultimately about the water, I could get it right. Every time. I would drag a stock tank into the sanctuary every week and boil a hundred kettles of water if dunking people in that tub meant they would automatically be faithful followers of Jesus. But baptism doesn't work that way.

Yes, the ritual is lovely—the profound words and the laying on of hands, and the rich symbolism. Yes, I love the water—all of it, as much of it as I can manage. But the truly essential part of baptism is the presence of the body of Christ. Whether we are immersed or poured over or sprinkled on, the water will soon dry. But the church will stay.

The pastor—even a five-foot-tall pastor like me—can manage to dunk anyone underwater by herself. But really, that's the easy part. It is infinitely more difficult to walk with people through life, to help them remain committed to the way of Jesus in this terribly un-Jesus-y world. That is a task that takes the whole church.

It turns out, for dunkers and sprinklers and even pourers, that what really matters is not the top of the head. Actually, it's not about any part of the baptized person's body. It's about the body of Christ—the alive, redeeming, gleaming holy body.

Torn

Rev. Julie Woods

We say we are torn when there is a choice to make.
We say we are torn when we are feeling indecisive.
We say I'm torn between the two—what shall I do?
I say, this is His body torn for you.

T orn is a word I use at the fraction (the breaking of bread)—not every time, but sometimes it just feels that *broken* is not enough; not quite the word I need. Because the table fellowship we share goes deeper than that. The bread itself is soft, yielding, and it doesn't break—you have to physically tear it apart. And so, when I lift it up to share, to show, to break, the natural words to use are, "This is his body, torn for you."

In the Scottish Presbyterian tradition, communion is not always frequent; in the last century it became positively infrequent—only twice, maybe three times per year. For some, so it remains—trooping up to church at the invitation of the kirk session (the church's governing body) to remember, as we were told to. In March and June and October—box ticked, duty done. To receive Jesus in tiny precut individual squares and

---

Rev. Julie Woods is a Church of Scotland parish minister, serving in Earlston, a village community in the Scottish Borders. Previously she served in a large urban parish in northeast Scotland. She is a regular contributor to *Spill the Beans* and the *Expository Times*. She blogs at julie-acountrygirl.blogspot.co.uk. She is the mother of three grown-up sons, and the stepmother of her beloved's four grown-up children. She loves being granny to Ellie, and spends any spare time she has creating fabulous meals for all who enter her kitchen.

to sip grape juice in a tiny prepoured individual cup. Because that's the way to do it, isn't it? Not to reconnect with what he did, but to sanitize it, to individualize it—not a corporate sharing, but you in your small corner and me in mine. And this is how it is done, and this is how some people prefer it—God in a box; nothing too demanding, nothing too real, nothing that speaks of discomfort or betrayal or death or dying.

For others, those formal services are anathema—regimented and impersonal. They prefer occasional gatherings, where the invitation is verbal, on short notice, and everyone who is there is there for the fellowship, not the duty. These gatherings do not take long, and do not have the formality of communion Sundays—but this does not make them informal. For to remember love and sacrifice and hope and family and fellowship and history and the unity that comes from such sharing can never really be informal, can it? *Informal* seems to indicate something casual or unofficial or careless, and communion is many things—but casual is not one of them. The very word *communion* implies community, coming together, sharing, and not individualized exclusivity.

These "other" communions may happen in church, or outside, or in someone's home, or at a hospital bedside; there may only be two people gathered, or a dozen. They are intimate and personal and the feelings shared go deep. Thus at these occasions I feel torn, torn between using the Book of Common Order and keeping some sense of formality and ceremony, or using my words, my story, to impart the depth of connection we feel as we remember, as we share, as we each tear off a small piece of bread and take and eat and taste. Together we experience the reality of Jesus among us.

What is happening during this time? Torn between traditions—is this a symbol, an act of remembering, a spiritual presence, partaking of Jesus's real body, real blood ... ? Do we sip or dip? Oh! The number of things we can be torn by when we begin to think about it, when we try to go deeper, when we seek truth and knowledge.

In the community I serve, although we do stick to our Presbyterian traditions of inviting the membership three times a year to come and share, we are also working toward reclaiming the real meaning of Christian community; we seek to share what it means for us to be in communion with each other. When I hurt, others hurt with me; when I weep, others shed tears too; and when I laugh and shout and reclaim God's awesome love—they are right there with me. We are moving out from the building, little by little; we go to the community, rather than always expecting them to come to us.

Jesus did not order us to build magnificent buildings with massive oak doors to shut people out. He commanded us to gather around a table and remember him—in bread and wine, the ordinary stuff of our lives. He gave us an example too: his final meal was inclusive. Everyone gathered—the betrayers and the lovers, the doubters and the deniers, the loyal and the fearful, all together, regardless. His table was for all back then, so our tables, wherever and whenever they are, are for all too.

I may occasionally feel torn, but mostly I feel communion with my sisters and brothers as we share this bread together; as we tear off a little piece of Jesus and remember that his story is our story, our history.

A Touch on Her Head

Rev. Martha Spong

I could hear the mother while I was still around the corner from the entrance to the neonatal intensive care unit. Her keening accompanied me in the required ritual of thorough hand-washing before I passed through the door. As it closed behind me, I could see instantly where I needed to go, to the huddle of stricken people in the corner: a middle-aged woman and a man of about twenty, neither trying to soothe or hold the new mother whose wail expressed their shared lament.

That night, I had been rushing to get dinner ready before a trustees meeting at 7. Just before 6, the phone rang. I stretched the cord to its limit, searching for a pencil to take notes. The volunteer chaplain on duty that night wanted help with a call from the NICU. A young woman had given birth to a baby at twenty-one weeks' gestation, not even old enough to inhabit the borderlands where doctors consider treatment, four weeks shy of the "very premature" date when they certainly will. The baby was alive, but not for long.

She told me all these things hurriedly. "I don't think I can do it," she said. "Will you go?"

Rev. Martha Spong is a United Church of Christ pastor and director of RevGal-BlogPals. She has served churches of many sizes and situations in Maine and Pennsylvania, specializing in intentional interim ministry. She writes prayers for pastors, adult curriculum, and preaching and liturgical resources, some of which she publishes on her blog, Reflectionary (marthaspong.com). Martha shares a manse full of books and yarn with her Presbyterian pastor wife, Rev. Kathryn Z. Johnston (also a contributor to *There's a Woman in the Pulpit*), and loves it when they have all four of their birds in the nest.

"Of course," I said, scribbling what little information she could give me on a scrap of paper. We didn't know each other well. She called me only because my name came first on the backup list. She didn't know that I had lost a baby in the same hospital.

I told my children to eat without me and kissed the top of my nine-year-old daughter's head, the one born after. "Oh Mom," she said, and shrugged me off, tossing her long hair. On the short drive to the hospital, I called a trustee from my cell to say I might be late to the meeting. A short fifteen minutes from the time I got the call, a nurse brought me sterilized water in a sealed container, which she opened carefully. She stood beside me while I spoke to the mother.

"I'm the chaplain. I've come to baptize your baby."

The mother was nineteen. I knew people would promise her there would be another baby someday, knew people would try to retell her story for her and make it "right," but where we stood there was no future, no hope, only a smaller-than-small baby girl with closed eyes and purple skin.

"We know that Jesus loved children," I said, "because when the disciples tried to keep them away, he said, 'Let the children come to me.' Baptism reminds us that we all belong to God; we are all God's beloved children. It is a sign of God's love and a promise that we will never be separated from God's love."

I'm not sure anyone heard what I was saying. I turned to the nurse and took the water, then poured some in my hand. I baptized the baby, Anne, in the name of the Father and of the Son and of the Holy Spirit. I touched her precious head. Anne's mother trembled beside me while the father and grandmother stood, seeming helpless to scale the walls of her grief.

Her sobbing rose again as I offered a closing prayer. At the nurse's prompting, I stepped away to fill out the hospital's baptismal certificate, a slim piece of evidence that God knew about a parent's love and loss, a paper promise that the dear, brief life would not go unmarked.

Anne died a few minutes later.

The baby I lost years before had only a funeral for a blessing, no baptismal touch on his head. We buried his ashes in the church garden and planted a dogwood tree there. I wanted to hear my pastor say his name, Christian, but it never happened. There are many ways people can fail to hold you.

I drove across town to church, just a few minutes late for the meeting. The trustees awaited me, a group of older, crusty, and inherently suspicious men. Each monthly meeting revolved around repetitive points of contention, from their suspicion of the "budget year-to-date" line on the financial reports to complaints about how many times the nursery school children flushed the toilet.

We don't tell each other about these things, the losses that happen outside safe and understandable boundaries. We don't hold each other, even though when we witness a baptism, we promise we will. We promise to love the child and support the parents. That's easy when everything goes smoothly.

"I've just come from the hospital," I told them, "and I can't stand for you to argue tonight." In an unaccustomed display of mercy, they did not. Instead, they listened to the story. They bore witness, and, although they never touched me, they held me that night as we prayed for Anne's mother.

I hope someone held her too.

Through the Eyes of a Child

Rev. Catherine MacDonald

Bright brown eyes peeked over the communion table at me as I finished placing multiple loaves of bread on it shortly before the World Communion Sunday service started. "Is that the bread we made yesterday?" he asked with wonder and awe in his voice.

I was newly ordained and eager to share all I had learned in my education and training; I was full of ideas for bringing the gospel to life in our time and place. I had shared a "Breads of the Peoples" communion liturgy with my session and proposed an all-ages bread-baking day. We could get to know each other in a setting that required participation and hands-on involvement, reflect on how bread was central to both body and soul, and begin to create shared memories and bonds that I hoped would deepen over time. My session agreed and we set the date for the Saturday before World Communion.

The chosen morning dawned. I had purchased the ingredients to make five different kinds of bread—cornbread, multigrain bread, pita bread, nut bread, and soda bread—each of them representing different peoples from

Rev. Catherine MacDonald is an ordained minister in the United Church of Canada. She presently serves at Saint Paul's United Church in Spryfield, Nova Scotia. She was previously the minister at United Memorial Church, Halifax, and Claremont United Church in Claremont, Ontario. She is the author of "Do You See What I See?" in *There's No ATM in the Wilderness: Daily Reflections for Lent*. She blogs at mywindowongodsworld.com. When not actively engaged in ministry, she delights in spending time with her husband and grandchildren, gardening, belly-dancing, and pursuing her recently discovered passion of exploring God's world through photography.

around the world. I had no idea how many people would show up. The only stipulation had been that you couldn't just drop your children off; it was an all-ages event.

First, one family arrived—both parents and two children. Then another family came, this time one parent and three children, then another, and another and another. Pretty soon there were twenty-five people, ranging in age from three to fifty-five. For a congregation whose average Sunday attendance was around forty, this was an amazing turnout.

We started by making a few batches of cinnamon biscuits, so that there would be a quick reward. Each child took a turn measuring, adding, and mixing ingredients and we popped the biscuits in the oven. Then we started making the multigrain and pita breads, which needed time to rise. Cooperation reigned that morning, with the adults each taking a group of children under their wing. We quickly discovered that it was better when family groups were separated.

As we measured, mixed, and kneaded, stories were incorporated into the breads: stories from the adults about how a mother or grandparent made bread, stories of the death of a mother in one woman's teenage years and never learning the skill and art of bread making with her, stories of living on a farm in England and having fresh bread with butter from the cows. I shared my story of Christmas baking with my sisters each year and heard the response, "We will be your sisters while you are here." We kneaded our stories together in the making of the bread.

Everyone took a turn kneading those two breads and they were set to rise. As we mixed the remaining quick breads, there was much disappointment from the children that these didn't need to be handled in the same way, that once the mixing was done, they could be popped in the oven and baked. The cinnamon biscuits were ready, but after sharing the sweet treat, the children got restless waiting for the next steps. One of the adults grabbed some old magazines and posterboard and set them to making a collage of bread pictures. The children told stories of their favorite breads and foods, stories of amazement at so many different kinds of bread, stories of surprise at how often bread was part of everyday meals and special ones, stories of connection and meaning.

The breads baked and cooled, the kitchen was cleaned and everything put away, and we dispersed to our separate homes and weekend tasks. The smells and images of the shared task lingered on, warming my heart with these beginning connections. Bread is so much more than simple nutrition; bread is community and home and family.

The next morning, the sanctuary buzzed with heightened energy as people saw all the bread displayed on the table. In the communion liturgy I'd chosen, there is a short definition of what each bread represents: cornbread, our native people; multigrain, with its blend of fibers and textures, for the justice seekers who bring all people together in an attempt to counter our culture of individualism; pita bread, the bread of the Middle East; nut bread, the bread of those who are considered irrational by our norms; soda bread, a quick-rising bread for those who need justice *now*. People are invited to choose the bread they connect with that morning. In my tradition, the United Church of Canada, children are welcome to the table no matter what their age. Each child approached the table with intense concentration and, without fail, each child chose a piece of the bread that he or she had helped make.

Jesus was known in the making and the baking of the bread. Jesus was known in the breaking of the bread.

🖋

A Prayer at Table

Rev. Karla Miller

We come to your table,
sometimes dressed in fine silver and linen cloths,
trays of tiny glass cups containing just a sip of blessing,
carefully cubed Wonder Bread, just a taste of love ...
We come to your table
sometimes swirled in batik and flowers and flickering
     flames of tealights,
sturdy earthenware goblets inviting deep gulps of promise,
crusty dense loaves torn in great chunks of new life ...
We come to your table,
with our dreams and hopes,
our cynicism and despair.
We come whether we believe a little
or a lot or not at all.
We still come.
Not knowing what to expect,
or expecting nothing,
we still come.

Rev. Karla Miller is a United Church of Christ pastor who knows the truth about cats and dogs, as she and her spouse, Liz, have opened their home in a Boston suburb to many rescues. She blogs at Amazing Bongoes (karlajeanmiller.blogspot. com). Her interests include art, people, politics, social issues, pocketbooks, shoes, shoes, chocolate, hiking, running, early evening when the sun is getting tired, discovering new music, playing with clay, and the Boston Red Sox.

We come because our lives are a wreck,
or at least pieces of them are a mess,
and we come because at least some of us believe love can
    conquer all.
We come to your table
for a sip of blessing,
a taste of love,
for a gulp of promise,
a chunk of life.
Or maybe we just come because it's nice ...
this bread,
this wine,
the very thought that it might be a little like heaven,
this sharing,
this table.
Your table.
Amen.

By Water and the Word

Rev. Jennifer Burns Lewis

> The Church's one foundation
> Is Jesus Christ her Lord;
> She is his new creation,
> By water and the Word.

I am a child of the church by adoption. From the time I was five, my mother, a nice Jewish girl who was a product of the boroughs of Brooklyn and Queens, New York, would take me to church. We would walk the quarter mile every Sunday morning. I've googled it. It seemed so much farther than that, as a child. It became my home away from home.

My mother chose that church for two reasons: she did not drive, and she found the preaching palatable. (She was a seeker from a culturally Jewish but nonpracticing family. I doubt we would have gone to a synagogue had one been within walking distance of our home in a bedroom community of New York City.) My mother, you see, was an agnostic, with a mind as sharp as a tack and a sincere prayer life. These are not mutually exclusive attributes. Not at all.

Rev. Jennifer Burns Lewis has been pastor and head of staff at the Presbyterian Church of Western Springs, Illinois, for over a decade. Ordained in 1983, she previously served churches in Illinois, New Jersey, and North Carolina. She blogs at anorientationofheart.blogspot.com, when she isn't walking her golden retriever, Lucy, or knitting socks, or enjoying rare time with her clergy spouse, Dan, or with her two young-adult children.

Alongside all her questions, wonderings, and petitions, she raised her only child to be a believer. I have vivid memories of standing on the pew next to her while she held open a hymnal, keeping our place with her finger, following each line of every stanza. I recall the colorful gladioli on the chancel table, a gift from the garden of the pastor with the forty-year tenure and a voice of reason and hope. He held my mother's questions and my childish heart. It was in that stark New England–style sanctuary that I was confirmed and baptized, received as a candidate for ordination, and ordained to the ministry of word and sacrament.

My mother sat in the front pew.

I remember my mother coming to hear me preach during my field education in seminary. I remember her eyes glistening with tears when we hugged afterward; she commented on my delivery, and just a little about the content.

Years later, after seminary, ordination, and my second call, one of my best friends from seminary and I realized we were in love. A child of the church by birth, my beloved is the son of Presbyterian elders; brother and uncle of elders, deacons, and seminarians; and grandson of a Welshman who jumped on a boat bound for the United States, where he attended Princeton Theological Seminary sixty years ahead of his grandson. My beloved is a native of Illinois. At the time of our courtship, he was serving a church in New Jersey and I one in North Carolina. That year he drove through the night for Thanksgiving with my family, who were visiting from out of town. We surprised them that day with his arrival and our friendship-turned-to-love. My mother's eyes were filled with tears. Six months later, my beloved and I were married at the church where I was serving.

My mother sat in the front pew.

Ten years later, my spouse, our two children, and I would find ourselves in Illinois, serving the church his Welsh grandfather had served during the Great Depression. One Christmas Eve, between services and after supper, my mother turned to me from the sofa. "You know, I've never been baptized." In fact, I had not known that. My mother had been a member of two Presbyterian churches. I guess no one ever asked.

Wearing my best "polity suit" (that is, knowing my denominational rules well), I suggested that we call the right people, receive approval, and baptize her in worship the next Sunday. She refused. At seventy, she was interested in admitting her baptism-free state to only a few. I removed the restrictive polity suit belt and mused, "Why don't we call just a couple of people you know and go to church with a bit early, before the 11 p.m. service?" She agreed. Gathered at the font in the church of my husband's and his father's baptisms, with my in-laws, my husband, our children, my stepfather, and my mother, I asked her the question from the Presbyterian Book of Order:

"Putting your whole trust in the grace and love of Jesus Christ, do you desire to be baptized?"

Tears in all of our eyes, she said, "I do."

I've never had a greater privilege than I did that night. It was out of order, illegal, a polity fail, but I would do it again in a heartbeat. We did not know then that my mother would die fairly suddenly just five years later, my last connection with my family of origin gone. But on that silent, holy night, amidst the glistening tears, we affirmed what we knew to be true, as I had the honor of saying, while making a watery cross on her forehead, "Susan Jane, daughter of the covenant, I baptize you in the name of the Father, the Son, and the Holy Spirit."

These days, I sit in the front pew and think of her.

Open Table,
No Reservations

Rev. Julia Seymour

> When an unbaptized person comes to the table seeking Christ's
> presence and is inadvertently communed, neither that person
> nor the ministers of Communion need be ashamed. Rather,
> Christ's gift of love and mercy to all is praised. That person is
> invited to learn the faith of the Church, be baptized, and there-
> after faithfully receive Holy Communion.[*]

I have thought about that phrase *inadvertently communed* many times over
the years. This passage, from my denomination's instructional document
on the sacraments, makes me feel antsy and rebellious. I've never inadvertently or accidentally communed anyone. I have always known what I was
doing—pressing bread into tiny palms, shaky fingers, sweaty grips, open
mouths, confident clutches, and doubtful grasps. Each time, I have said a
version of "The body of Christ, given for you" with an honest look into the
face of the person I was serving. There was nothing inadvert about my
actions.

Rev. Julia Seymour has been the ordained minister at Lutheran Church of Hope
in Anchorage, Alaska, since August 2008. She believes strongly in ecumenical and
interfaith cooperation. She blogs at lutheranjulia.blogspot.com. Julia enjoys reading, writing, crochet, and outdoor activities. She lives with her husband, their two
young children, and their devoted Labrador retriever.

My predecessor at the first congregation I served had begun discussions about open communion. He did offer communion to older children, but there was still a very formal first communion. Typically between first and third grade, children would be taught about communion and then have the opportunity to take their first communion surrounded by their family and by the community's prayers.

I supported the idea of communion education for that age group (and older), but I still was handing out the body of Christ willy-nilly around the altar. Every hand stretched out received. Everybody was welcome to come forward with open hands. If God has no barriers to grace, why would I erect them?

More to the point, how could I *enforce* barriers? Is there a hierarchy in the sacraments that I did not know or understand? Perhaps baptism confers some mystical ability to perceive the presence of Christ in communion and I have been circumventing that. If I have been, I was not doing it inadvertently.

In that first congregation, there was a woman in her late forties named Annabelle. She had some serious mental and emotional disabilities, but was genuinely embraced by the community. Her parents were very elderly, but when Annabelle stayed with them for the weekend, she came to church too. It was clear that she loved to be there and her voice could be heard rising above the congregation during the Lord's Prayer and other corporate response times.

Annabelle always enthusiastically approached the altar rail. Her parents had worked for decades to teach her "proper" responses to various events, including and especially receiving Holy Communion. Yet her enthusiasm for all things often overrode the lessons she had been carefully taught.

One Sunday, I handed Annabelle a piece of bread and said, "The body of Christ, given for you."

She plucked the host from my fingers with her own and stuffed it in her mouth, grinning at me and blurting out, "Don't mind if I do."

I grinned back. Her parents were horrified, but I thought it was the best and most enthusiastic possible response to Christ's invitation to communion and community. *Don't mind if I do.* Rather than groveling in the face of grace, Annabelle reveled in it. I loved this.

Suddenly, I knew that was my response to communing all people. "Don't mind if I do." Some people are washed on their way to the communion table. Others may eat their way to the font. There is no way of containing the movement of the Spirit, and it flows between both of these holy and mysterious gathering areas. In all things, I do my best to examine what I'm doing because, in truth, I want to be sure I am not in God's way. Gratitude expressed to me for a welcome or openness in the congregation's practice is not personal when I hear it. But it is the blessed assurance that the Spirit is moving and I've managed not to impede the flow or the experience.

The paragraph at the beginning of this chapter is still the official stance of the denomination into which I have been ordained. It is also (still) in the constitution of the congregation I serve, though we do not follow it with any strictness. In truth, communing anyone and everyone is my most flagrantly disobedient act. And I do it regularly. I know that I have communed and do commune unbaptized people. I've never done it inadvertently. And I don't mind if I do.

🖊

---

* Holy Communion, Application 37G, *The Use of the Means of Grace*, Evangelical Lutheran Church in America.

God Gives Us Life

Rev. Jemma Allen

I am standing outside the neonatal unit of a university hospital in Beijing. In one hand is my phone; in the other a liturgy:

> Our help is in the name of the Eternal God
> Who is making the heavens and earth.

Two Chinese men come and stand less than a meter away, openly curious about the *laowai*, the foreigner, the only one to be seen today on the hospital grounds. The temperature hovers around freezing.

Inside the neonatal unit lies the youngest member of our congregation. His father and I are praying, as we do each afternoon. At this hospital, parents are allowed to stop by once a day, buzzed into the otherwise inaccessible building. They have a few minutes to visit with a nurse to get an update on their child. For three weeks, two days, and twenty-one hours, these parents won't see their son. Their much-loved son, born early, struggling to breathe and to eat.

And so I am standing outside the ward. Today the boy's father is in his office on the other side of the city. He will make a phone call to the hospital for news of his child, but I am here on the hospital grounds and

Rev. Jemma Allen is the associate priest at All Saints Anglican Church in Howick (Auckland, New Zealand), where she is responsible for ministry with children, young people, and their families. She formerly served as co-pastor of the Congregation of the Good Shepherd in Beijing, China. She blogs at exilicchaplain. wordpress.com. Her sanity strategies include knitting socks, loving dogs, skyping friends, and eating veggies.

we will pray together by phone. We read scripture and then, as the curious bystanders watch, I extend my hand and pray the same words of blessing we pray each day, blessing the child, praying for the doctors and nurses. Praying that the love of God, the love of his parents, the love of his family will somehow pass through the concrete walls and be perceived by that tiny baby, doing his best to breathe and eat and grow strong enough to go home.

For the first week of his life, it is impossible for me to call any member of the congregation about anything at all without causing hearts to leap into mouths in case it is news from the hospital. They have loved him and prayed for him long before they will ever see his face.

At three weeks, two days, and twenty-one hours, the baby is wrapped in a bundle of quilts and goes home. The member of the congregation who drives dad and son home reports it as a nerve-racking trip—navigating a busy city with a very tiny baby on board. The joyful reunion of mother and son eclipses every moment of anxiety. There are tears. Of course there are tears.

Spring comes. In China one hundred days of life is a milestone. It is an occasion for celebration, in some places for the formal giving of the child's name. This family celebrates with a restaurant dinner: many tables of friends and colleagues eat and drink and celebrate that we are together with this wee baby one hundred days from that perilous birth. I am allowed to hold him briefly—his mother's mother is convinced to relinquish him for a few minutes so that I will not be entirely unfamiliar to him when I hold him at his baptism the next morning.

And so it is, on his 101st day, that we come to be standing in front of one of his families: the congregation in Beijing where his parents belong. There are more people than usual—a small number of baptism guests and as many of the congregation as are in the city, making a particular effort to be present for this high and holy day in the life of our community.

This baby had been in the hospital through Advent. Every time we prayed, "Lord, we are the people who long to see your face," we thought at the same time of that baby, hidden away inside the hospital, and how much his mum and his dad and all of his family longed to see his face. And now, ready for us to pour water on and anoint with oil, to bless, and name, and proclaim God's love to, there is a bright, shining baby face.

There are tears. Of course there are tears. They begin even before the opening hymn as the choir members practice their song of blessing. Family members cry. Even the ones who don't understand English and don't know exactly why they're crying cry.

My voice is mostly steady. I say the opening words of the baptism liturgy, and at that moment I feel an easy and great certainty:

God is love; God gives us life.

That love is so present in this moment, the love that has sustained these parents through the waiting, the longing, the anxiety: their love for one another and this big love that has held them up; the love that this group of people feel for this small child. We are not related to him by blood, but by that love and by our hope.

The liturgy continues:

We love because God first loves us.
In baptism God declares that love;
In Christ God calls us to respond.

There is water and oil. There are promises made, blessings offered, support declared. And as we conclude, we pray:

May he grow to love, worship, and serve you, and bring life
    to the world.

The *amen* we say is not the amen of a future, may-it-be-so hope, but a certain amen—it *is* so.

Such a small baby.

He has already brought such love and life to our world.

Hostessing

Rev. Monica Thompson Smith

To term my usual kitchen activities *hostessing* would significantly upgrade them. I prepare the same breakfast I made yesterday and the day before that, and then do the dishes. I prepare lunches that appear remarkably similar to the lunches I made yesterday and wash those dishes too. I prepare a slightly-more-varied, kindergartner- and preschooler-approved supper and—you guessed it—wash the dishes. It doesn't *feel* like hostessing; it *feels* insignificant and monotonous. But, gradually, sneaking up on me without awareness and certainly without my intention or invitation, feelings of adequacy and even competence have infiltrated my work in the kitchen. At times, I catch myself *enjoying* the act of preparing a meal. Though my inner feminist quibbles with me about this, it feels natural and right as I cook for my family.

When I stand behind the communion table, those feelings of competence and rightness accompany me, even when, in truth, I have no idea what I'm doing on a practical level, nor can I comprehend what mysteries my hands touch. I'm a supply preacher who occasionally gets invited to serve communion. Each congregation choreographs the sacrament a bit differently, and they are not always able to articulate the intricacies of their customs. I tend to improvise, whisper hurried questions, and take my cues from the congregation's reactions.

Rev. Monica Thompson Smith is a stay-at-home mom and a regular supply preacher. Most recently, she served as minister at Good Shepherd Presbyterian Church in San Antonio, Texas. She is a host(ess) of the popular 11th Hour Preacher Party at revgalblogpals.org. She is married to a United Methodist minister, and they have two Presby-dist/Metho-terian daughters.

Which is how I found myself standing in a cow pasture, with a (very distracting) longhorn behind me and a communion table in front of me. The table—bread, juice, chalice, plate, and all—was covered with a pristine white tablecloth, not theologically required by our Presbyterian tradition, but necessary in this case, to keep the multitude of flies away. The elders who would serve the elements stood in a semicircle around the table. Without even a first thought, much less a second, I reached out to remove the tablecloth and fold it. They immediately all leaped forward with shock on their faces and stopped me. One of them gasped a little. Another said, in a whisper, "That's *our* job."

That gave me pause. After all, I have gotten accustomed to being responsible for almost any table-related task, whether at home or at church. I wasn't used to the cloth being atop the elements, but it was their usual practice, even indoors. I hadn't thought about it beyond "That needs to come off." Nor had I considered that it would be someone else's task to remove and fold the cloth, rather than my own.

There I stood, in the place of the host(ess), proclaiming to the gathered body of Christ that Jesus himself was the host of this meal, and I felt somehow disconnected from what my instincts, both theological and quotidian, told me was my job as a hostess. After worship, the congregation encouraged me likewise to be a guest at the church picnic, to enjoy the food and fellowship, while other people took care of the hostessing.

Next to the table, I bless and break and pour as a hostess. And then I open my hands to receive those same gifts of grace as a guest. I handle the visible means and proclaim an invisible grace to myself, as well as to the congregation. I eat the supper that has been prepared at the Lord's Table in this dual role of hostess and guest. I suspect that most preachers and presiders have to puzzle out how to weave those roles together.

But, I wonder, do all ministers experience the intersection and resonance between the roles of host(ess) at home and host(ess) at the Lord's Table? On a good day at home, I can sense the presence of the Holy in our kitchen, around our table. We extend grace and forgiveness as we share the macaroni and cheese and eschew the green beans. Our time together nourishes our bodies and our souls as our meal binds us together.

I carry those familial bonds with me at the communion table, as I extend Christ's grace and forgiveness to those gathered around it. I carry, too, the comfort in my role as hostess that has grown alongside my marriage and family. My hands are practiced as I fold white napkins and break bread and pour juice. My mind and spirit are thus freed to contemplate the mysteries of grace received without measure, of the body of Christ bound together in the sacrament, of precious souls entrusted, if only temporarily, to my care. And, in turn, that body holds me as I return home to the mundane—but no less sacred—meals of our kitchen, where I contemplate those very same mysteries.

Three Sisters

Rev. Bromleigh McCleneghan

I've always been glad to be a part of a tradition that baptizes infants. Wesleyans have our moments of works-righteousness, but when you baptize infants, when there's really nothing that helpless, nonverbal individual can do to earn anything, you can't help but be reminded that God loves us, loves them, not for anything we've done or refrained from doing, not from any understanding or accomplishment, but simply because it is in the nature of God to love us, and it is the desire of God to know and welcome us. "An outward sign of an inward grace," we say. Water simply makes plain what is already true, and has always been: that we are God's, and we are beloved.

This spring, a woman who had grown up overseas in a country with a majority non-Christian population, and a state religion, started worshipping with us. She'd come to the States for grad school and found her way to us in her mid-thirties. The architecture in our large university chapel never fails to inspire folks of all traditions: there's something about the air, the light through the windows, the silence, and the way the sound of the organ fills the place. I, who never went to church in college, found my way

---

Rev. Bromleigh McCleneghan is ordained as a United Methodist minister and currently works at Rockefeller Memorial Chapel at the University of Chicago. Her first book, *Hopes and Fears: Everyday Theology for New Parents and Other Tired, Anxious People*, was cowritten with her friend and colleague Rev. Lee Hull Moses. Bromleigh blogs at Love and a Cough (bromleighm.com). A preacher's kid, wife, mom of two, and sister of sisters, she likes to read, write, cook, eat at restaurants, and go to plays. She would give anything for just one more bathroom in her house.

back after a summer in Europe of visiting cathedrals and feeling, for the first time ever, moved to pray on my own. I get it, about the space.

One day this woman asked me how she should go about becoming a Christian. We celebrate a very open table, so she'd already communed with the congregation, but it nonetheless seemed obvious to liturgically minded me that what she was looking for was to be baptized.

We set up a time to meet, so I could get to know her better, so I could speak to her about this desire to become a Christian. She assured me it would not cause any problems with her family, who did not support the government's form of religion in her country of origin.

She knew next to nothing about Christianity. I gave her some books I thought might be helpful, but though her spoken English was beautiful, she much preferred to read in her native language.

I tried to explain the Trinity; the life, death, and resurrection of Jesus; the story of sin and reconciliation and redemption. I tried to explain the church and our sacraments.

It took fewer sessions than I would have imagined.

She was curious about rituals—are there prayers that must be prayed? Times of day that rituals must be observed? Are their duties and obligations? *Not really ...*

I felt initially that I was letting her down, wondering if I should have sent her to the Episcopal or Lutheran church down the street, both of whose pastors had more experience catechizing adults. But it was enough for her; coming from a tradition with prescribed practices, she loved the idea that she could connect with God—that she could seek and experience God—in her own words, in her own time.

Every baptism before I got to my current position was done in the midst of worship, in the midst of the body of Christ. But she did not want to be baptized during worship. She is very reserved, and this seemed to her a deeply personal, and thus deeply private, moment. This would eventually be between her and the community, but in this moment, her baptism was about her and God.

She came to the church on Easter Eve. I had my six-year-old with me, and she served as a witness. The three of us gathered in the chancel, around the altar and the beautiful big blue art glass bowl we had purchased for such occasions.

I performed the liturgy, asked if she accepted Christ, if she would turn away from sin and work to resist evil and injustice in all its forms. I feared that I was asking her to promise things I hadn't fully explained.

But she said yes, so I cupped water in my hand, once, twice, three times, and I baptized her in the name of the triune God. I called her beloved—beloved to me and beloved to God. I said to my daughter, "This is the miracle of baptism—I am still your mother, but all three of us are now sisters too, sisters in Christ, sisters in God's family."

I hugged the woman, and she kissed my daughter on the top of her head. The grown-up ladies wept a little, while my daughter had this look of confusion and wonder on her face, as though she knew something important had just happened, but she wasn't exactly sure what it was or how to describe it. With my years of theological training and pastoral practice, I was probably wearing a similar expression.

The Worst Communion Ever

Rev. Martha Spong

We started making plans for a RevGals get-together before we knew what we wanted it to look like, how many people might come, or even where it might be. We had some dreams, but mostly they amounted to a glorified slumber party. We had a little money, but not enough to hire a notable speaker. Everything seemed hypothetical to the point of delusion, including the name I coined: the "Big Event."

Hotels charged for meeting space, and most retreat centers would not allow alcohol, which seemed to bother some of us. Finally, someone made a ridiculous suggestion: we could go on a cruise.

I had never been on a cruise. I was the serious-minded mother of three children. How could I leave them for four nights and be completely out of touch, in international waters? It seemed far too hedonistic for a group of lady ministers. It also seemed, however, that we could get meeting space for free. The debate ended. A cruise it would be.

Rev. Martha Spong is a United Church of Christ pastor and director of RevGal-BlogPals. She has served churches of many sizes and situations in Maine and Pennsylvania, specializing in intentional interim ministry. She writes prayers for pastors, adult curriculum, and preaching and liturgical resources, some of which she publishes on her blog, Reflectionary (marthaspong.com). Martha shares a manse full of books and yarn with her Presbyterian pastor wife, Rev. Kathryn Z. Johnston (also a contributor to *There's a Woman in the Pulpit*), and loves it when they have all four of their birds in the nest.

The week after Easter, we arrived in New Orleans from all over the United States and even England. I boarded the ship as leader of RevGal-BlogPals, but had only the barest thoughts about how to make people feel welcome, which was too bad, considering how few of the twenty of us knew each other in person. Our name tags had to include our blogging pseudonyms. (*So that's what Songbird looks like!*)

We spent the first day digging deeper into our life stories while the ship crossed the Gulf of Mexico. I bemoaned the seventh grader at my house who found fault with everything: the Worst Birthday Ever. The Worst Thanksgiving Ever. The. Worst. Fourth of July. Ever.

I confess to you: I dropped the first f-bomb, setting the stage for something more like a 1970s feminist encounter group than a church retreat.

Our wonderful presenter, eager to support an ecumenical ministry for clergywomen, had us each choose a card with a word we would contemplate throughout the program. Mine was *play*—but how could I play when I felt so anxious about making sure everything went well? We had most of the second day off to explore Cozumel. Back on the ship, we partook of the midnight buffet, featuring (hedonism alert) champagne jelly in which nestled tiny raspberries and perfect candied violets. Our group looked happy. They found the disco and danced and laughed. I continued to fret, however, about whether things were going well, to reexamine all my conversations and rate them on my daughter's scale.

The next day, the ship turned back across the Gulf and, like kids on the last day of camp, people lamented our short time together. I'd even gotten the length wrong.

Someone said, "It's too bad we can't celebrate communion."

Rats. Another thing I hadn't thought about ahead of time. Still, I asked, "Why can't we?"

The immediate gathered group raised concerns about who would lead the service. "I'm Presbyterian," someone said. "I would have needed to arrange it with my session." "Well, I'm Episcopal," said someone else, "and I would need the permission of the bishop of ... wherever we are."

Finally, I felt free to get something right. "I'm United Church of Christ," I said. "I don't need anyone's permission!"

We asked the cruise staff for bread, juice, and wine. Who could serve with me, without permission? I thought immediately of Amy, one of our

Episcopal bloggers. The story of her frustrated ordination process in a conflicted diocese grieved us all; she seemed so clearly gifted for ministry. Others had the same thought. As the day went on, one after another in our group came and whispered in my ear, "You should ask Amy."

After dinner, we gathered not in the Upper Room, but in the card room, all the tables for four rearranged into one big rectangle.

It could have been the Worst Communion Ever, accompanied as we were by the partying sounds of the last night at sea pouring from every bar on the ship. It could have been the Worst Communion Ever, as we had no prepared liturgy. It could have been The. Worst. Communion. Ever—as the loaf promised by the purser turned out to be twelve slices of white bread stacked precariously on a plate.

We gathered around the tables-become-Table. I took a breath and told a playful story. "That night must have felt like the worst communion ever," I said, "interrupted by betrayal and arrest." I invited stories of our time together. We laughed and prayed and cried. I tore pieces of bread to place in dear hands. Some dipped them in the juice held by Methodist Sarah, and others drank from the cup of wine Episcopal Amy held, ministering to us as one of us. For those few minutes, we let go of how we did things on shore. Even me.

It may have been the Best Communion Ever.

Ashes to Angels

Ministry and Death

> [God] will wipe every tear from their eyes.
> Death will be no more;
> mourning and crying and pain will be no more,
> for the first things have passed away.
>
> REVELATION 21:4

Where there is life, there will also be death.

We serve in the privileged and humbling position of being a welcomed stranger in the rituals and moments of death and dying. Working as clergy gives us an honor few others will gain. We go by different titles: priest, minister, pastor, mother. Whatever you call us, one thing remains: we will be there to love and hold, to whisper and pray; to communicate God in the midst of sorrow and grief.

We arrive abruptly, but quietly; we come into tragedy or turmoil; we sit in long silence, watching and waiting for peace to descend.

We serve in churches and hospitals, in hospices and nursing homes; we minister in cities, suburbs, and the countryside. We go wherever God calls us; and, if we can, we offer comfort. Our stories are as distinct as we are, each uniquely made, each uniquely known. And yet, our stories are also the same, for we strive to communicate God: we offer the love, compassion, and peace of Mother, Son, and Spirit in a myriad of different places and situations. When death comes, there may be a smile or a tear, and both are equally welcomed. The end of this story is just the beginning of the next.

The Weight of Ash

Rev. Deborah Lewis

It's an odd and intimate gesture, brushing someone's hair aside to mark her with death.

One college student comes forward eagerly, yet awkwardly, aware of the strange intimacy of the moment, hungry for it but a little antsy to have it behind him and to be back in his pew. His vulnerability shows like a tag sticking up from the back of his T-shirt, visible to others before he realizes it himself. He reminds me of myself my first year after seminary, when I almost gasped and cried as the priest touched my forehead. I was single, living three states away from my family, and it was the first time I'd been touched in months. The priest moved my bangs aside and it was that gesture as much as the ashes themselves that broke through to me. I felt like a person again, physically connected to other people, even if just for a brief moment.

Many Ash Wednesdays after that one, I try to remember my embarrassing need and surprise that year. The Spirit blew in where words and touch comingle, offering sighs and solace deeper than either. I don't completely understand it—what happened to me that time or what happens each time we move into the ritual—but I remember it. I trust it.

Rev. Deborah Lewis is an ordained elder in the United Methodist Church and currently serves as campus minister for the Wesley Foundation at the University of Virginia. While working for nonprofits in the region, including the Appalachia Service Project, she discovered her love for Appalachia. She's currently learning a lot about autism and love from her stepson. Deborah and her husband, Woody Sherman, root for the Washington Nationals and enjoy a good road trip. She blogs at Snow Day (deborahlewis.net).

The physicality of this ritual grounds it. Ash may not seem sturdy enough to handle this weight, but it's a perfect reminder of the mutability and transformation we experience at God's hands. I wait in the front of the sanctuary, holding in my hands a pottery bowl I made, which, in turn, holds the ashes—dust, holding clay, holding ashes. Working with clay reminds me of our own provenance and destination. We come from earth, effort, love, and breath. We are called to follow in the wake of Christ and, eventually, to return to earth's dust.

I'm relieved I have only one line to say. It leaves room for the mystery of God in the midst of ash, oil, and skin. I resist filling the space with reassuring nods and smiles or any false attempts to make the whole thing less weird and intimate. My role is simple and intense. I hold a space for the wild weirdness of God as I hold a bowl of earth and smear it into each person's skin.

Gritty midnight-black ash, slick with olive oil, rubbed into the shape of a cross, refuses to be tidy, trailing ash across cheeks and the bridge of a nose. Suddenly it's the most obvious thing about each of us, right out front, the first thing we see now. *This is what you are. Remember? This is what you will be in the end. Remember.*

These out-of-the-ordinary middle-of-the-week services attract a different crowd from our Sunday morning regulars. The dark cold of February pushes the small group together in the shadowy sanctuary, huddled and expectant. Tonight we are the oldest members of the congregation, smoke-scented homeless men up from the temporary shelter in our basement, a man in military uniform, and unwrinkled students largely unfamiliar with death. Even when death has been close in my own life, as it has been this year, it startles me with its bluntness and probability as I mark the forehead of the military man. I picture him headed to a war zone. *Remember that you are dust, and to dust you shall return.* Of course these are not mere words. They are true for each of us, in the most literal, non-symbolic way. The military man makes it harder to miss this essential fact and I wonder if he hears this blessing as promise or threat or both. How do any of us hear it?

Some people close their eyes as I reach out with the ashes. Some look up expectantly and full of trust, like baby birds ready to take what is dropped into their open beaks. It would be easier not to look closely as they come forward. It would require less of me if I let my eyes glaze slightly and focused only on the forehead, divorcing it from the rest of the face and body.

We're used to distant transactions like that, staring past the cashier, making deposits at the bank, placing an order in a café. I could do that here.

But that's not the call. Before I turn to dust again, this is where I stand, at the intersection of flesh and spirit, word and action, human and divine. I pray that I won't steel myself against the flood of sensation and love I feel as I watch each one pause, receive my touch, listen for God's reminder, and walk away marked. *This is whose you are. Remember.*

Before the Resurrection

Rev. Joanna Harader

After the bone marrow transplant, Lola's cancer was under control and her body was getting stronger ... until it wasn't. Easter found us gathered for an early worship service in Lola's hospital room.

We had plenty of hymnals to go around, but somehow it hadn't occurred to any of us to bring a Bible. If we had been at a Motel 6, we could have grabbed one from the nightstand drawer, but apparently the Holy Book is harder to come by in a hospital. The nurse was sure she could find one, but in the meantime I thought, *I'm a pastor. It's the Easter story. I got this.*

"On that morning so long ago, three days after seeing Jesus die an agonizing death, the women headed to the tomb. Joanna and the Marys and the others did not huddle in grief; they prepared the spices and went to the grave. They were willing to face death; to walk into the tomb, pull back the grave clothes, and gently, with bare hands, rub spices onto the skin of Jesus's slowly rotting flesh."

I told the whole Easter story that morning to Lola and everyone gathered there. The glowing men, the empty tomb, the good news spread to the other disciples. I didn't even use the Bible when the nurse finally brought it. I know this story. This is the foundational story of my faith. The resurrection holds the promise on which I have staked my life.

Rev. Joanna Harader serves as pastor of Peace Mennonite Church in Lawrence, Kansas. She lives with her mother (Rev. Cheryl Harader, also a contributor to *There's a Woman in the Pulpit*), husband, three children, two dogs, two cats, two cockatiels, five chickens, and a hamster. And yes, sometimes she has to hide in her bedroom to get any writing done.

But that year the story stopped for me with the women and the spices in that moment before they saw the angels. The story stopped with their faithful intention to enter into death's space with love, with their willingness to look at death, to touch it, to be present with it.

Because that's where we all were. We knew Lola was dying, and we were angry and afraid and so very sad. But we came anyway. We entered the room; we looked at her; we touched her. And we sang. We had hymnals instead of oils and spices, so we anointed her with music, letting the sacred words and holy harmonies cleanse us all.

I wish that the Gospels told us more about those days, those hours, after Christ's death and before the empty grave. I wish I knew more about those women—all their names and what they did to prepare the spices and how cold they were that early dawn as they walked toward the tomb.

As Christians—and especially as Christian *preachers*—we take from this Easter story the mandate to share the good news. But I find my calling is just as often to navigate the spaces in between crucifixion and resurrection; to prepare the spices and walk unflinchingly toward death; to look and touch and be present with whatever horrors people face.

My own father, a pastor and chaplain, had the liturgical sense to walk us through his death within the confines of Lent. His was a sudden, startling illness that moved the story from a doctor's office to the hospice floor to the funeral home in about a month.

And I will tell you the truth. During that month, it was the women with spices who I longed to have by my side. The friends who brought food and sat in the waiting room with our kids. The people who held me and whispered, "I love you." The chaplains who said simply, "I am so sorry. This is awful. I am here."

I believe the resurrection is real. I believe Lola and my dad have eternal life in God. I believe I will be with them again someday. I believe all of it— all that good news. I believe it and I rest in it and I breathe it in … deeply.

Still, just like that Easter in Lola's hospital room, in the wake of my father's death I find that I want to stay with the women as they prepare to visit the tomb. I want to dwell in those moments before they see the glowing men, before they know that Jesus is alive. I need this in-between space.

Ultimately, life has conquered death, yes. But death is still very much a part of life. In the face of that reality, I want to be with—and I want to be one of—those women. I want to do what needs to be done in the face of tragedy. I want to be willing to walk toward the hard realities. I want to be brave enough to enter death's space and reach out my hands in love. I want to anoint the dying (which is all of us, really) with oil or spices or hymns or whatever will make this flesh-and-blood life as close to holy as it can be.

From the Pen of the Hospital Chaplain

Rev. Liz Crumlish

With all the equipment silenced, no hiss of oxygen mask, no alarming pump drivers or monitors, just the comforting sound of slow, shallow breaths, peace descended.

There was noise from the other side of the wall, where families were visiting with loved ones. There were footsteps and hushed voices in the corridor. But in this room, tucked around the corner, a room that was often used for the privacy of death, there was a curious stillness. A stillness born of inevitability, but also of mystery.

I took Margaret's hand and settled in to wait.

There were no relatives, and the few friends who hadn't predeceased her were too frail and infirm to sit with her. At that moment, I had nowhere else to be except at the bedside of this saint as she took her dying breaths. I did not know her story, was not privy to the details of her life up to this point. And, in that moment, it did not matter.

All that was needed was a companion on the road, a fellow traveler beside whom to rest awhile as that threshold was crossed and life on this side was relinquished for whatever lay ahead. During the course of the next few hours, from time to time, Margaret held out her hand and smiled

---

Rev. Liz Crumlish is a Scottish Presbyterian minister living and working on the west coast of Scotland. She has worked as a hospital chaplain and now serves as a parish minister. She loves to spend time walking on the beach, processing thoughts and writing in her head, with the stunning scenery of Scotland as a backdrop.

83

beatifically at something only she could see in the corner of the room. But, for the most part, she simply rested while her life force ebbed away oh so gently, with occasional sighs and long pauses between breaths.

I sensed it before I saw it. That moment of death. That letting go of her hold on this life and taking up the life that lay before her.

It was like discarding an old, comfortable sweatshirt in favor of a flirty dress.

And I was grateful that I was there, that I was the one privileged to be allowed to ease her over that border between life and death, grateful that she did not struggle but drifted purposefully on to the next phase of her journey, reclaiming her vitality, entering a space where my company was no longer required. Knowing her spirit was gone, I took my leave, content that I had fulfilled my calling in that moment.

Such a contrast to the night before—a welcome contrast—to the trauma of the emergency department where two young parents, nearly children themselves, awaited my arrival in a corridor teeming with urgency and pain. They waited in the corridor because their child's untimely death was now a matter for inquiry and probing and judgment by the authorities, and they were banished beyond the boundaries.

No peaceful sighs or beatific smiles for them.

Not even quiet respect for their bereavement; instead, invasive questions and demands to recount events over and over again.

So they, who had discovered their still, lifeless child and had lovingly wrapped her and brought her to the hospital, hoping desperately to awaken from the nightmare in which they were trapped, were no longer allowed to tenderly caress her breathless form, to stroke her cheek and go on attempting to will life back into her.

No quiet corner room for them, or for the relatives who arrived in force to offer support.

No hushed voices or silenced alarms, but full frontal human trauma on every side.

No sense of inevitability and purpose and the rightness of timing.

Just gut-wrenching helplessness and hopelessness.

And yet as I sat with them on a hard plastic chair in a corridor that bore scuff marks from trolleys laden with all kinds of brokenness, in that moment too, I knew a sense of fulfillment: the assurance that God's call involved being helpless and mostly silent but nonetheless present in the midst of such tragedy. Called to be a nonanxious presence, a point of reference, even, in moments, an advocate for these young parents as they struggled with the protocol of sudden death and searing loss. Called to find a way to bring calm into a room filled with so much intrusion—from family, from medics, from police.

Called to negotiate time and space to perform the last offices of love.

Negotiating the good-bye that these parents were denied.

Negotiating the opportunity to be a trusted caregiver whose presence would ensure that no policies were compromised while they finally were allowed to spend some time with their beloved angel child.

Out of the melee that continued in the corridor.

Away from the raw, loud grief of loved ones.

Accompanying them as they traversed the path of sacredness.

And as they gazed with love and with loss on her lifeless form—though it pierced me to the core—in that moment, I knew the call of God and the reality of the incarnation.

The Moses Basket

Rev. Elizabeth Evans Hagan

On a Tuesday afternoon while I was sitting among liturgy books and daydreaming about what I'd cook for supper, I got a call from the local funeral home.

A baby was dead.

"How old?" I asked the funeral director. He called me for the "hard" deaths in families that had no pastor. The last funeral I led for him was a teen suicide.

"Oh, only three weeks old. The baby boy developed some muscular disease and just couldn't make it. He died peacefully at home. So sad. So very sad. But, luckily this wasn't the mother's first child. He had a two-year-old brother."

My heart sank.

Not only was "Luckily, this wasn't the mother's first child" such an insensitive thing to say, but I was all too familiar with infant deaths. My husband and I were in our third year of trying unsuccessfully to have a baby. I'd already endured two miscarriages.

"I've already told the mother about you," the director went on. "She seemed really happy that you're a female pastor."

Rev. Elizabeth Evans Hagan is an American Baptist pastor. She previously served as senior pastor at Washington Plaza Baptist Church in Reston, Virginia. Her articles have appeared on the *Associated Baptist Press*, *Ethics Daily*, and *Christian Century* websites. She blogs at Preacher on the Plaza (elizabethhagan.com). She is married to Kevin and together they love collecting airline miles.

Immediately, I knew I was in, like it or not. The question would be, how could I get through the service without sobbing?

I got on Facebook right away and asked several colleagues for advice. All were speechless. Most volunteered to pray for me as I prepared.

So, I felt that I was on my own. I pieced together the words of a funeral service over the next couple of days.

An hour before the service began, I shoved a granola bar in my mouth in place of a dinner I didn't feel like eating. I took my robe from the vestry closet. I printed out my sermon. I marked the readings in my Bible. I got in my car and drove the five miles down the street.

Walking into the funeral home, I opened the door and noticed how heavily I was breathing. Soon the parents arrived. *No chance to back out now!*

The dad stood coldly before me in his pressed navy suit. The mother wiped away her tears with the cuff of her black striped shirt. She paused to stare off into space and then let me know she would be speaking at the beginning of the service.

"I'm glad you feel like sharing," I offered.

The mother nodded and walked away. She couldn't look me in the eye. I understood.

Standing by the back door of the chapel, I saw the pews were full. After looking over my sermon notes just one more time, I said a quick "Help me, Jesus" prayer as I moved toward the crowd. The two-year-old brother ran uncontrollably in circles around the pews. The organist had already started playing. No flowers adorned the front of the room. Instead, as I moved closer, I saw a basket on the altar—a woven brown basket like those that fill the aisles at international craft fairs. As I walked down the center aisle, it became clear exactly what was inside: not cards of tribute, not stuffed toys or a blanket, but the baby himself, the dead baby I was about to eulogize.

As I forced myself to peer in, I noticed that his face was pale, with a peaceful expression. Baby boy was dressed in a white sailor suit with white booties. You'd think he was just taking a nap.

But he wasn't taking a nap.

I choked. I really choked once this all registered. I was about to do a funeral for a dead baby—a real live dead baby.

To enter the pulpit area, I needed to walk to the left, in front of where the immediate family sat. It seemed right to hug this grieving mom one last time. She whispered in my ear: "Don't you like the Moses basket? I picked it out myself."

I tried to smile as I thought of how Moses's mother made a basket so she could give away her son too. I stepped into the pulpit and kept my gaze on the crowd. I would get through this funeral by *not* looking at the dead baby.

Near the end of the service, we'd reached the time to say the Lord's Prayer, but I couldn't quite go there yet. Though I am not a solo kind of singer, most certainly not at funerals, somehow the words of "Amazing Grace" came to my lips and had nowhere to go but out from me. If amazing grace couldn't cover the public and private tears of women like this mother and me, I didn't know how we could all go on. Some of the congregation joined in, but with the mostly unchurched crowd unsure of protocol, many looked confused. Yet I couldn't stop.

There were no answers for this grieving family, or for mine, either. There was hardly comfort in those moments. Three-week-old babies shouldn't die. Nor should seven-week-old babies in utero, like mine. But they did.

Old Man's Hand

Rev. Martha Spong

I came home and found a blinking light on my answering machine. Mr. Morton's son had left a message: Would I come to the hospital, to intensive care? The family had a meeting with the doctor, and Mrs. Morton wanted her pastor to be there.

Three years before, I had met the Mortons on my first home visit as a newly ordained pastor. I was the first woman installed to serve their church. I drove two towns over to the tidy mobile home park where they lived in retirement. He had just turned ninety, a little man, perhaps five-foot-four-inches tall. They no longer attended church, but he typed postcards every month to send to radio stations and newspapers, advertising our church's roast beef supper. She was eighty-six and seemed frail to me. Their neatly kept home, decorated in shades of brown and tan, contained evidence of how they kept their minds lively, with a complicated jigsaw puzzle in progress and books of jumbles handy on every side table. They told stories of childhood hijinks and how they met; of his job at a car dealership, moving vehicles from one city to another; of living a happy,

---

Rev. Martha Spong is a United Church of Christ pastor and director of RevGal-BlogPals. She has served churches of many sizes and situations in Maine and Pennsylvania, specializing in intentional interim ministry. She writes prayers for pastors, adult curriculum, and preaching and liturgical resources, some of which she publishes on her blog, Reflectionary (marthaspong.com). Martha shares a manse full of books and yarn with her Presbyterian pastor wife, Rev. Kathryn Z. Johnston (also a contributor to *There's a Woman in the Pulpit*), and loves it when they have all four of their birds in the nest.

faithful life without much money. They invited me to the kitchen table for coffee and cake.

Many visits followed. I would go home with jumbles in my purse.

When Mr. Morton slipped while shoveling snow on Christmas night the following year, I brought him a prayer shawl made with my own hands. Bruised, he rebounded, but in the new year Mrs. Morton had a series of unexplained nosebleeds. Their sons convinced them to move back into town, to senior apartments near the church. They proudly gave me a tour of their new space, praising the large closets and the convenience of the kitchen. Her health worried him, but she remained unconcerned, trusting his care.

They lived in the apartment for a year filled with more ambulance rides for her. He turned ninety-three and seemed fine until a sudden hospitalization the day before I came home to their son's message.

Seated in a wheelchair to make navigating the hospital easier, Mrs. Morton waited with her two sons in a small, awkward room with too many chairs, set apart for such discussions. The sons assured me they went to church, just not mine, an odd thing people do when they meet their parents' pastor. The doctor arrived and explained the sudden illness that could not be reversed. He related the prognosis and the wishes Mr. Morton had recorded in his living will. Mother and sons agreed that he would not want to be sustained by machines. They turned to me for something— relief? Blessing? I gave what I could, and after the doctor left the room, we prayed together.

I expected to go with them to a bedside vigil, but after the *amen*, the sons announced a decision made before I arrived. They would take their mother home. They whisked Mrs. Morton away, wheels turning swiftly, before I could say good-bye to her.

They jumbled me.

The nurses in intensive care were less surprised than I to see the family vanish. They knew more about human nature, more about disappointment, more about self-preservation. It might not happen soon, they warned. It might be all night.

I spent a summer as a chaplain resident in the same hospital, sat at bedsides listening, stood witness at a deathbed. As a local pastor, I volunteered for overnight on-calls, prayed with a wife who couldn't see that her husband was already dead, counseled a doctor trying to convince a mother to take her son off a ventilator, and even broke up a fight in the hallway. Those people passed through my life in an hour or a weekend. I didn't know the colors of their curtains, or whether they preferred landscape photographs to works of art in jigsaw form. I could not leave dear Mr. Morton there alone.

Sitting at Mr. Morton's bedside, I thought of my parents, the day each had died, my presence with one and my unwanted absence from the other. I read aloud from the Psalms, but grew self-conscious, so I closed the Bible and looked at the monitors measuring his fading vital signs. He made quiet efforts now, working the puzzle of life and death alone.

I watched his face and remembered his voice. He was the talker, the one who told me how they met while she smiled her remembrance.

I took his hand, not much bigger than my small one. The skin felt like tissue paper. His own mother once held this hand, when it was new and curling. He used it to throw balls, to pick blueberries, to drive a car, to drive many cars for many miles for work and for pleasure.

This hand solved jumbles, crosswords, jigsaws. This hand served me cake.

I loosened my grip just a little, but he tightened his, not quite finished. So I sat, waiting for the last piece to be placed.

One Saving Grace

Rev. Anna Scherer

"Don't worry. I'm not leading it and we don't have to do anything." That's what I said when I told my husband that we needed to stop by the church one Saturday evening for a memorial service.

A woman in the neighborhood had requested that my church host a memorial service for her father. Jane had asked an outside minister to perform the service; she just wanted to use our sanctuary because it was large and nearby. My boss asked me to "babysit" the service—to be there to unlock things, turn on the lights and sound system, and make sure everything went smoothly. I called and talked to Jane for a few minutes the week before the service.

When we showed up at the church, I found out that a friend of ours had been hired to play the harp before the service. She set up her harp while I unlocked things. Neither Jane nor the officiating minister had arrived yet, which wasn't too worrying because I was early.

Time passed and people started to show up. A woman came to me and told me that she had been asked to sing during the service. She had a cassette tape that she wanted to play as her accompaniment. This was the first I had heard of these plans, and the church sound system couldn't play a cassette tape. Fortunately, my husband found a tape player and

---

Rev. Anna Scherer is an Episcopal priest. She graduated from Virginia Theological Seminary in 2009. Although she has lived in various places in Texas and Belize, she now considers Virginia her home. Her blog is Not Graceful but Grace-filled at oneofgrace.com. She aims to make new mistakes instead of repeating old ones.

jerry-rigged it to play next to a microphone. Meanwhile, I kept trying to reach Jane on her cell phone. No answer. I left messages.

The situation slowly went from normal to concerning, to worrying, to panic-inducing as the planned start time of the service came and went without either Jane or the minister.

The harpist continued to play much longer than she had intended. The woman who was to sing suggested she go ahead and do so. She sang a few praise songs, and in between said words of praise and prayer. I was grateful.

Jane showed up forty-five minutes *after* the memorial service was supposed to begin. I asked her where the minister was.

"Why don't you just do the service?"

I was completely caught off guard by the request, but decided to make the best of it and quickly pull a few things together. I picked one of the scripture recommendations from the burial service and asked Jane to read it. I thanked God profusely for the Book of Common Prayer.

I went to the pulpit and read a few prayers from the burial service liturgy. Then Jane started to read the short passage from the Christian scriptures that I had asked her to.

Then she kept reading past the end of the passage.

Then she started to add her own commentary interspersed with the reading.

She praised my church for leaving its doors unlocked at night ... so that homeless people can sleep in the pews. (While my church does leave the doors to the sanctuary unlocked, it is so that people can come in and pray. We aren't equipped to serve as a homeless shelter!)

Then the commentary started to get kind of personal.

Her father, she said, was faithful to her mother his whole life, and never cheated.

Her parents, she said, were virgins when they got married.

That was why, she said, she was still a virgin, and still looking for the right man.

I was sitting up at the front of the church and turned my face away from the congregation so that they wouldn't see the look of horror on my face. I didn't know how to stop things. Eventually, Jane paused for a bit and I got up and said some prayers and ended the service.

As people left, I was more than relieved that the service was over and that people were incredibly polite and made no mention of anything being strange. I wanted to tell folks that this service wasn't representative of my congregation or of me, but I didn't want to be the one to call attention to what had occurred or cause people to stay even longer. Jane was obviously in distress over her father's death and likely was grappling with other issues in her life.

I did check in with my husband and my harpist friend to make sure that I wasn't imagining what had happened. It certainly was the most remarkable experience I've had of a funeral, and a lesson in being prepared for the unexpected and unplanned.

My one saving grace is that I found out a couple of days later that the widow's hearing aids had been off and she didn't hear a word that was said.

A Million Little Deaths
A Prayer

Rev. Karla Miller

Every day we die a million little deaths.
Every day we have the promise of a million little
    resurrections.
O God of life and death,
when, pastoring,
we get lost in the despair
of broken relationships,
tragedy,
illness,
long-suffering pain,
a final breath,
a life taken,
hold us in the abyss of grief and desolation.
Be the ground upon which we lie,
shuddering with cries too deep for words.
Let us sink into you.

Rev. Karla Miller is a United Church of Christ pastor who knows the truth about cats and dogs, as she and her spouse, Liz, have opened their home in a Boston suburb to many rescues. She blogs at Amazing Bongoes (karlajeanmiller.blogspot. com). Her interests include art, people, politics, social issues, pocketbooks, shoes, shoes, chocolate, hiking, running, early evening when the sun is getting tired, discovering new music, playing with clay, and the Boston Red Sox.

O God of life and death,
Embrace us in the multitude of collapses we bear each day:
when we betray or are betrayed,
when we make a mistake,
lose our center,
and forget who and whose we are—
just to name a few.
O God of life and death,
We pray for the courage to open our tear-filled eyes,
a resurrection in and of itself.
Help us to know the hands that hold us are Life,
the eyes that behold us are Love,
the feet that walk beside us are Hope.
Every day we die a million little deaths.
Every day we have the promise of a million little
    resurrections.
Amen.

Life Disrupted

Rev. Deb Vaughn

I remember driving home that morning and thinking, *What day is it?* In my chaplain's world of fluorescent lights, there was no demarcation between the lines on the calendar.

Somewhere around 10:30 p.m. the previous night, a young man was pronounced dead in the emergency department. He had sustained multiple gunshot wounds to the chest at close range and had massive blood loss. I made eye contact with the charge nurse. "Family's on the way in," she said.

This was not the first time I would sit in the grief room with a family. But it was among the hardest. The relatives gathered, six in all, and I came in with the doctor and the charge nurse. The doctor said no more than, "We did everything we could, but ..." and was cut off by the screams of three of the women. They ran out of the room. The young man's mother and two men stayed to listen.

After several minutes of officially explaining "what happened," the two staff members left, and I stayed with the family.

Rev. Deb Vaughn is ordained as an American Baptist pastor and works as a professional interfaith chaplain for JSSA (Jewish Social Services Agency) in Montgomery County, Maryland. Formerly she worked at George Washington University Hospital and Shady Grove Adventist Hospital as a chaplain, and on the pastoral staff of churches in the Washington, D.C., area. She is author of several articles for the ViewPoint section of the *Christian Feminism Today* website (www.eewc.com/viewpoint) and blogs at An Unfinished Symphony (unfinsymphony.wordpress.com). She bakes a mean loaf of bread, and is a rabid Ohio State Buckeyes football fan.

In the street below us, we could hear the continued screams and cries of the women who had left, now outside on the sidewalk below. The mother looked at the two men. "You go to them," she said. "Get them home. I'll come home in a cab in a bit." At her insistence, they left.

Again we sat in silence. I have learned as a chaplain: *wait ... pray ... wait ...*

Finally she turned to me and said, "He just finished tenth grade. Tenth grade! He started going with those boys and ..."

She broke off and looked at me, suddenly guarded. "Your kids ever been in a gang? Get shot at?"

"No," I said quietly.

"Then you don't know," she said. She glared at me. "You are safe in your suburb, your kids in good schools ... You don't know!"

More silence. What could I say?

Her shoulders were shaking as she wept. My mind whirled. I was painfully aware of the privilege of birth and the racial gap between us. Though my life was far from sheltered, it was nonetheless true that I did not fear for my children's safety on a daily basis.

Finally I responded. "I see it happen here all too often. Stories that no one knows, horrible stories. And it's why I'm still here."

She continued to weep.

"Tell me about him," I said. "Tell me what he loved, what he was like ..."

Tears rolling, she told me about his stuffed blue dinosaur. How he hated thunder, "even as a big boy." How he wouldn't wear anything but jeans, and could do math problems in his head.

She pulled out her phone and showed me pictures. Goofing around with his sisters, wearing their hats, shoes, and sunglasses. Standing in front of the Martin Luther King Jr. Memorial.

"He wanted to be a big man, big like MLK," she said. "Instead ... he ran with those ... punks. Those damn gangs. They spend their days trying to shoot each other. I just don't know ... I feel like my life just got disrupted ..."

"It is that," I said. "Disrupted."

She blew her nose and looked over. "You gonna tell me everything is gonna be OK?"

"No."

Her face was incredulous. "No? *No*?"

"No, I can't tell you it's going to be OK. It's never going to be the same. It's going to be hard, especially these next few weeks."

She sat back and took a deep breath. "Yes. Yes it is." She reached for my hand and said, "I don't mean to yell. But I don't know what to do with all this pain. God knows, I don't."

We sat in silence, holding hands, as the fluorescent lights buzzed overhead. I started to sing "Precious Lord, Take My Hand," softly ... at first alone, and then she joined me, our voices breaking with sadness.

"I don't know if I can do this," she sighed.

We sat together. Tears would come and go.

Finally, the precinct's detective came in and said he needed to interview the mother alone. She said quietly but firmly, "No. I need my chaplain with me. By the grace of God, she's getting me through this."

We sat a while longer. I prayed. She answered questions. When it was time for her to leave, she turned to me and hugged me. "I hurt so bad, chaplain, so bad. I hope you never know how this feels ..."

I fell on my bed the next morning, and cried as I fell asleep. There is so much evil and violence in this world that I do not understand. But even life disrupted is indeed a life held together by God's grace.

Of Facebook
and Angels

Rev. Julia Seymour

Bzzzzz. Bzzzzz. The phone signaled that I had a text message. I executed the nineteen-point turn necessary to roll over in bed at thirty-four weeks' pregnant. As I grasped the phone, the glowing screen belied the darkness of the message: *The baby didn't make it.*

Gasping, I sat up and texted back, *What?* The friend on the other end spilled out the details of the events of the evening. Our mutual friend, Sarah, had gone into early labor last night. As it turned out, the baby had a birth defect that was incompatible with life, but it had not yet been detected. The baby was born and had died all in that December night.

I rubbed my own abdomen and ached for Sarah. We were part of a group of women with babies all due in January. We'd had one preemie, born in October, but he was doing well against all odds. Now our small group had a loss. I couldn't stop crying, praying, sniffling, feeling helpless.

In the morning, we gathered online to discuss how we could help. *I wish I could be there with her* was the most common sentiment, typed over and over in our chat boxes. None of us lived near each other, but we had made a community through websites and then through Facebook.

Rev. Julia Seymour has been the ordained minister at Lutheran Church of Hope in Anchorage, Alaska, since August 2008. She believes strongly in ecumenical and interfaith cooperation. She blogs at lutheranjulia.blogspot.com. Julia enjoys reading, writing, crochet, and outdoor activities. She lives with her husband, their two young children, and their devoted Labrador retriever.

Twenty-eight of us knew each other's scares, frustrations, our potential names, and our hopes. Sarah's loss was our loss.

She said no to the chaplain, one woman typed. *She only wants you, Julia.*

I wish I could be there. My fingers flew over the keyboard. *Alaska is a long way from Idaho.*

I cried in grief and helplessness. As a pastor, I was used to sitting with people in pain. I had learned to conquer the need to "do" or to "fix." Yet this was so different—it felt too close. This was my friend—yes, a friend I only knew online, but someone whose pain was as real to me as if we'd been in-person friends for years.

In my agitated state, I placed a prayer request for my friend and for myself in the RevGalBlogPals Facebook group. *Please direct some prayers toward Idaho for my friend who lost a baby at thirty-six weeks last night. Peace for her and her partner and for me, at thirty-four weeks myself.* I stared at the screen as the promises and assurances of prayer appeared.

Then, *plink,* I had a message. RevGal Marci Glass of Idaho asked where my friend was and if she could be of help. I hesitated only briefly before responding. Marci told me that she could easily visit my friend the next day after church. *Please,* I said. *Please go for me.*

Relief flooded my body. I could help. I could send an emissary, a different member of the body, shining with the same Spirit, in my stead. It seemed only fitting that I was sending someone I trusted and valued as a colleague whom I also knew through the wires and waves of the Internet.

When Sarah tells the birth story of her baby, there is sadness and grief. Then she speaks of community—of nurses and midwives, of friends and family. And then, she pauses. *Julia sent an angel named Marci who came to us, baptized our baby, and prayed for us.* Marci's visit is part of the story, part of the facts and the truth of those events.

The Internet, Facebook, blogs, Twitter—they are not monoliths of anonymous power. They are potential bridges of hope, healing, and hospitality. In this dark, dark moment of Sarah's life, help came. It came through communities of like-minded people who dared to be vulnerable and trusting with one another. It came through a willingness to share pain, to ask for help, and to volunteer to close the gap.

I know, theologically, that angels are beings created by God—apart from humans. Yet I am not entirely sure that we do not occasionally inhabit the same space. For brief moments, we make connections in life in which we imbibe the heady air of heavenly proximity. On that December day, I heard the brush of wings as I typed. A hospital hall in Idaho echoed with the footsteps of one child of God going to greet another.

They Don't Teach
That in Seminary

What We Learned
Through Experience

The law of the Lord is perfect,
reviving the soul;
the decrees of the Lord are sure,
making wise the simple.

PSALM 19:7–9

W e arrived at our churches prepared: our minds full of theological terms, our hearts filled with passionate ideals, our boxes overflowing with books and a freshly framed diploma and a hot-off-the-presses certificate of ordination balanced on top.

But there are at least 393 things they don't teach in seminary.

That's the number of stamps it takes to put additional postage on 131 church newsletters declared by the post office not overweight but improperly oriented for first-class postage. Of course there is no such thing as a thirteen-cent stamp to be had when this happens, nor a ten and three combination. From the vault, a postal worker will retrieve 131 American Toleware five-cent stamps and 262 four-cent Chippendale Chair stamps, a daunting sight. Seeing as it is Optimum Newsletter Arrival Day Eve, a faithful pastor may find herself standing at a counter, placing the stamps one by one, all 393 of them.

One hopes she will learn these valuable lessons:

1. It probably could have waited until the next day. Really.

2. We don't have to do everything ourselves. When lovely church members heard this true story the next day, one after another said, "Why didn't you call me? Surely you had other things to do!" Surely, and verily, we do.

3. Our indispensability is a myth.

4. Still, we are sometimes powerless not to do it that way again.

5. Don't be in such a hurry to change things. Consult the postal (and other) rules first.

6. When we can't get out of our own way—and that will happen—remember that Jesus felt that way too sometimes, and got out of everybody's way, praying in the wilderness or napping in the back of the boat.

7. We all continue to discover gaps in our education. No one meant to leave these things out in the classrooms or over lunch. We're all still learning too.

8. Lastly, we will absolutely live and learn at least 393 more things about the intersection of the sacred and the ordinary, about church keys and lost plungers and missed flights and the mysterious way a knock at the door interrupts the gospel story and manifests it at the same time.

The Pastor's View

Rev. Diane M. Roth

Sometimes I have an almost uncontrollable urge to take a picture while I am standing in front of my congregation. I am not sure exactly why that is, but I will be standing there, singing or getting ready to pray or making an announcement, and suddenly something will occur to me. I realize that I have a unique view—the pastor's view. No one else sees worship exactly the way I do.

One Sunday a few years ago we were singing the opening hymn and I was thinking that, even though the church was not totally full, it looked like a pretty good crowd out there. A little later, when everyone sat down, we seemed smaller again. I was a touch disappointed. Which view was the true one?

Why does the church look bigger when we are standing? I wondered. This must Mean Something, but I was not yet sure what.

Sometimes, I do love the pastor's view. We were singing the hymn "Jesus Shall Reign," and as we began to sing the words of verse three, "and infant voices shall proclaim / their early blessing on his name," I caught the eye of a young father who had his baby daughter in his arms. He smiled at

---

Rev. Diane M. Roth is a Lutheran pastor currently serving at Woodlake Lutheran Church in Richfield, Minnesota. Previously she pastored three small rural churches in northeastern South Dakota: Bethlehem, Naples, and Our Savior's. She blogs at Faith in Community (faithincommunity.blogspot.com) and writes for "Living by the Word" in the *Christian Century*. In her spare time, she reads, walks her dog, knits, and checks out new restaurants with her husband.

her, and then looked at me in that "you-too-know-the-secret-handshake" sort of way.

Other times the pastor's view breaks my heart. Once I saw an older couple lean into each other and begin to cry. We were singing "Soon and Very Soon" and had just gotten to the verse, "No more dyin' there." I knew that they were remembering their only daughter, who had died.

Sometimes I notice an absence when I look out over the congregation. Once I ran into a fairly new member of our congregation at the grocery store. After just a few months, I had observed that she was suddenly not in worship anymore. She told me that she had to work three jobs to make ends meet. She didn't know when she would be able to return. Regret and weariness showed on her face. How could it be that I was, until then, unaware that the Sabbath command was not just a matter of personal piety, but also a matter of justice, denied to some?

Sometimes it is a presence I notice when I look out over the congregation. A couple comes back to worship after a long time away: he has just been diagnosed with cancer. A teenager comes to church alone and sees none of her family in church, but slips in next to her mother's best friend. If only all the children in our congregation knew this ease.

A couple of years ago, an early November ice storm rolled in over Saturday night and into Sunday morning. I feared I would be disheartened by the small numbers, even though I knew roads were hazardous and the danger was real. Yet when I looked out over the congregation, the few I saw included every generation—grandmothers and babies, teenagers and widowers, enough children for a children's sermon, enough people to sing with good courage.

The pastor's view is not the only legitimate one. Yet, somehow, the pastor's view is as essential as it is unique. I stand up on Sunday morning and I see this collection of individuals. Some of them are here early every week. Some sneak in late and sit in the back. Some of them walk from across the street and some of them drive many miles, even in bad weather. I see some strangers, and I see some people I know so well, whose joys and pains I have shared. I see children who dance and fold their hands in earnest prayer. I see people who look at me with pleading longing: will I give them something to hope for today? I see a happy, overwhelmed couple with a newborn son, and a widower grieving his wife. I stand up and welcome everyone, and sometimes I think, *It seems like a small crowd this morning.*

But then they stand up, and they get a lot bigger. I wonder why that is. It is one of my jobs to think about it.

Maybe it's this: When we stand up, we are not just a collection of individuals. When we stand up, we are a choir, a work crew, a family. We are a team of mountain climbers, a band of wandering disciples.

People of God, no matter how small you are, you are bigger when you are standing up, together.

What They Will Remember

Rev. Jan Edmiston

Although many seminaries offer a course in boundary training, this training tends to focus on issues like dating parishioners (don't) or embezzling church funds (really don't). There is little to nothing offered about Personal Life Boundaries. At what point does a single pastor inform her congregations that she is seriously dating someone? At what point—if ever—does she share that she takes antidepressants? What if a church member receives a fatal prognosis on the day of her sister's bridal shower?

After my first year in a rural parish in upstate New York, as a single twenty-something living in the fishbowl that is life in a village of four hundred souls, I had become obsessed with my need for a vacation. One of my seminary friends had a parishioner with a vacation home in the Caribbean and a group of us had been invited to stay in that heavenly beachfront abode for free. Free. All we had to do was pay for the flight and show up. My expectantly pounding and lonely heart could barely wait for that Saturday when I would fly south to spend a glorious seven days with friends whom I had not seen in months.

But on the Friday before that Saturday, Thelma Vandecastle died.

Rev. Jan Edmiston is associate executive presbyter for ministry in the Presbytery of Chicago in the Presbyterian Church (USA). She previously served as pastor of Fairlington Presbyterian Church in Alexandria, Virginia. She has written articles for both *Congregations Magazine* and *Homiletics*, and she regularly speaks on shifting church culture for twenty-first-century ministry. Her blog is A Church for Starving Artists (achurchforstarvingartists.wordpress.com). Her favorite names are Fred, Ben, Jay, and Libby.

Thelma didn't just die. She died while running off the worship bulletin on the mimeograph in her red-and-white kitchen. Technically, she didn't die until after the ambulance reached the hospital, but once she tripped on that mimeograph machine cord and crashed into the wall headfirst, it was just a matter of time. And when she died, so did my hopes for a vacation.

I had paid for the (no-possibility-of-cancellation-with-reimbursement) airline tickets, but Thelma Vandecastle was dead, and her sister—the oldest member of the congregation and Thelma's housemate—wanted a Sunday afternoon funeral. Everything in me wanted to be sipping adult drinks on the beach that Sunday afternoon with people who had known me since before ordination.

My response to this request was what you might call an emotional breakdown, in the comfort and privacy of the church manse.

While my soul and body ached for a vacation far, far away, I was utterly torn. This was Thelma Vandecastle, the closest thing we had to a church secretary. And—for the love of God—she fell while running off the church bulletin. I called a seasoned pastor down the road, hoping against hope that he would tell me to go ahead and catch my flight to the islands. But he didn't.

"If you stay for Thelma's funeral, the congregation will remember for a long time. If you leave, they'll remember even longer."

I stayed. I ate the ticket cost and then bought a replacement ticket that I couldn't afford. And while the vacation was lovely, it wasn't as restful as I'd hoped. Seminarians are told that church service will involve personal sacrifices, but nobody tells you that it will be like this.

Over the course of my professional ministry, there have been choices between a family reunion and the wedding of a church leader's daughter; between going to my mother's deathbed and the funeral of a beloved young adult member; between my own child's last senior game on the lacrosse field and a crucial meeting of the personnel committee. And the truth is that people will remember for a long time which choices we make, and we will be judged on those choices. If you stay for one person's funeral, you have to stay for everyone's funeral because *that's what they will remember* after you go.

We clergy were never taught to serve with an eye on what will happen after we leave. But the pastors who follow us will be impacted by some of the choices we make during our tenure. I have a friend whose predecessor in the parish was independently wealthy and she had returned her entire paycheck to the congregation each month during her years of service as the pastor. She will always be remembered for this, above all else. But she wrecked it for the pastor who followed her because the congregation was miffed to learn that he would actually need his paycheck to support his family, thank you very much.

When I worked seven days a week for my congregation and relinquished sabbath days and vacations—for Thelma Vandecastle and others—I made life terribly difficult for the pastor who followed me, especially when he insisted on taking Fridays *and* Saturdays off. He might be remembered as a slacker while I might be remembered as a martyr. Both are caricatures, of course, and yet remembering human beings as caricatures is often our specialty in the church.

What if, instead, we clergy strove to be remembered for modeling healthy spiritual lives to our people? What if we modeled our ministry by looking at the future—not only for how we will be remembered but also for the sake of those coming after us?

Locks, Doors, a Walk-in Safe, and the Keys of the Kingdom

Rev. Jennifer Garrison Brownell

> And I tell you, you are Peter, and on this rock I will build my church, and the gates of Hades will not prevail against it. I will give you the keys of the kingdom of heaven, and whatever you bind on earth will be bound in heaven, and whatever you loose on earth will be loosed in heaven.
>
> MATTHEW 16:18–19

In seminary I learned, among about a gazillion other things, to read the words of Paul Tillich, to speak in public without puking beforehand, and to recognize that my experience growing up in a church where women frequently served as pastors was a unique blessing. Most of all, I learned to keep confidences.

Keeping confidences is so important that it is one of the promises made at ordination, along with studying the Bible and administering

---

Rev. Jennifer Garrison Brownell is pastor at Hillsdale Community Church (UCC) in Portland, Oregon. She received a master of divinity degree from Seattle University's School of Theology and Ministry. Jennifer is the author of *Swim, Ride, Run, Breathe: How I Lost a Triathlon and Caught My Breath*, and she blogs at There Is a River (46thpsalm.blogspot.com). Jennifer lives in the suburbs behind a purple door with her husband, his wheelchair, their teenage son, and two unruly pooches.

sacraments. Keeping confidences is so important that not keeping them is not called *losing* them, as you might think, since losing is usually considered the opposite of keeping, but *breaking*—as in, destruction.

I take this vow seriously. But I'm pretty sure it's not breaking a confidence to tell you that Marian made the *best* sandwiches. Not all nonagenarians are really up to sandwich making, let alone delivering, but that's what she did. Sometimes we'd arrive to find them wrapped in wax paper in the church's fridge with a staff person's name written on each one, so we'd know whose was whose.

Among the gazillion-and-one things I did *not* learn in seminary was the secret code to determine who receives a key, and therefore after-hours access, to the church building. The treasurer has a key, naturally. So do members of the committee who set up the receptions and clean up after them. But does the occasional delivery of sandwiches to a staff of three merit a key? And if it does not, whose job was it to ask Marian to turn in hers? If it was my job, I did not fulfill it. Those were really great sandwiches.

Marian not only had a key, but she also knew the combination that opened the walk-in safe in the basement. I don't know about you, but I'd never seen a walk-in safe in a church before. Almost everyone who sees it for the first time is surprised by the bank vault–looking door in the otherwise innocuous hallway to the classroom wing. Even if the first-time passerby doesn't actually *say* it, I can see the question floating around in a little thought bubble. *Wait, what? Why does a church need a walk-in safe?*

The first time I passed the vault was the day I interviewed to be the congregation's pastor and I blurted the question right out. It was a day for questions, after all. The answer, compared to the candor I experienced the rest of that interview day, was uncharacteristically vague.

"Oh, just a bunch of musty old ... Nothing ... *You* don't want to ..."

By the time I got someone to open the safe for me, a few months had passed since my first day, and a few more doors had been opened. By then, I had heard three stories of betrayal; listened to a father describe his proudest moment with his teenagers; stood on a windy hillside at sunset saying good-bye to a very old woman; and held the hand of a man who was dying what we usually call "too young." By then, I had overheard more than a few people fret about the future of the church, giggled over tea at Marian's house, and prayed with the committee charged with distributing mission funds.

You arrive the first day and it's all locked doors and walk-in safes and you think you'll never crack the code. You think you'll never figure out who gets the keys and the combinations and, when it comes to the church building, maybe you never will. I still don't know why a congregation of 120 modest souls needs a walk-in safe, or why some people need keys to the building and others don't. I probably never will, just as I probably will never understand why we keep what we do in the safe.

After the long months of waiting, when I finally walked inside, the contents were underwhelming to say the least: a few boxes of old financial records, a carton of tea cups someone had donated to the church a few years back, and, over in the corner, a pile of hangers saved from the last rummage sale.

In seminary, I learned how to keep confidences, and, ten years in, every day I'm learning why. Locked away behind the doors of hearts, unlike the vault in the basement, are dazzling jewels and priceless treasures. With every conversation, every story, every encounter, it's like I've been given the keys to a vast and beautiful kingdom and, with them, the astonishing ability to loose what has, until now, been bound.

The Good Samaritan Test

Rev. Sharon M. Temple

I went to seminary because I've loved Sunday school since infancy. I grew up on stories like the familiar tale of the Good Samaritan, told by Jesus. How many times did I hear that story told in Sunday school classes when we opened our Bibles to Luke 10:29–37? How many coloring sheets and crossword puzzles pictured the man left to die by the side of the road? How many Vacation Bible School skits featured the unbelievable scenario that not one, not two, but *three* people did not stop and help the critically injured man? How often were we young disciples relieved when the Good Samaritan stopped and saw the man's need? Yes, we knew the Samaritan—stranger and foreigner and the unlikely definition of good neighbor. He rescued the man, and he saved our faith.

As a Sunday school child or youth group youth, I could have aced a Good Samaritan test. We were told that we would face tests. They were called "tests of faith," those pivotal life moments when God sets up a test to determine how strong our faith is. We would either keep the faith or let it slip away. When we learned the Lord's Prayer, we learned to pray for deliverance from times of being tested. Avoiding the test would be ideal.

At age thirty-two, a few years before I started seminary, the Good Samaritan test showed up one day in my life, like a pop quiz. We had been

---

Rev. Sharon M. Temple served as interim pastor at Central Saint Matthew United Church of Christ in New Orleans after having served seven congregations in Dayton, Ohio, and northeast Pennsylvania. She blogs at revmama.com. She enjoys traveling anywhere, gardening, hiking, playing with her two grandsons, and laughing with friends and family.

taught to always be the Good Samaritan. Unfortunately, in this scenario, I was the one disabled on the road.

That Sunday, thirty years ago, I was driving home from church, past a restaurant where many of my fellow church members went for Sunday dinner. My car died so suddenly that I barely got it into the restaurant parking lot. My six-year-old daughter was with me, and I was eight months pregnant. In July. At noon. In Texas.

I gathered up my young daughter and we went into the restaurant, looking for a phone. I made several calls to the few friends whose phone numbers I could remember. No one could come and help us.

One of those futile phone calls was to my own church, where I was a Sunday school teacher and active layperson. I had just worshipped there minutes before. There was a mission committee meeting in progress. Fortunately, someone answered the church phone. Unfortunately, he said no one could come until after the meeting ended, and they were just getting started!

I was stranded and overwhelmed. I was holding back tears and trying not to let my daughter see how worried I was. We were hungry, and I had no money.

As I repeatedly made those calls, I could see church members eating their meals in the restaurant. Not wanting to be rude or interrupt them with my sad story, I tried to be inconspicuous and not stare in their direction. Several of them—days and weeks later—would ask me if I was having some trouble that day. They had wondered among themselves if something might have been wrong.

While I unsuccessfully tried to dream up some rescue options, in full view of these apparently concerned church members, a stranger approached us and asked if we needed help. He tried to put us at ease. He gave us his name and business card. He introduced his wife. When he offered to give us a ride back to church, we gratefully accepted.

The Good Samaritan story had come to us, and all those we encountered played their roles, just as Jesus said. Church people passed by the one in need. An unlikely stranger noticed and responded. I was the innocent, stranded, incapacitated one. The church people were guilty, and I harshly judged them for their failure.

The Good Samaritan story was taught again in seminary. We learned to translate it from the Greek, to exegete it, to teach it, to preach it. We passed those seminary tests. We were ready to teach effectively, preach brilliantly, and lead church members to never, ever leave anyone by the side of the road.

That test comes back again and again. Will I be the one to notice, and stop, and help?

Just yesterday, on the church steps, there sat three new Tulane University students, lost and stranded in the heat, unable to get transportation. I was distracted, and I almost passed by.

Almost.

As I drove them to get their first tattoos, these young women, neuroscience majors, said they had never met a woman pastor before. They were glad I came along when I did.

They were excited to call their parents and tell them that they'd let a stranger give them a ride.

Only Four Letters

Gillian Hoyer

After a ten-hour shift at the homeless shelter, I say to clients, "Bye, I'll see you tomorrow," and then hop on my bicycle.

I pass the Seventh Day Adventist church. More often than not, a group of folks who will not go to the homeless shelter huddle under the cover of its large front porch with their shopping carts fully laden. They are tightly wrapped in the sleeping bags we were giving out last week to everyone we had to turn away from the shelter because we were at capacity.

As I round the corner, I pass one of the many Anglican churches in town. There are already a few people tucked in near the locked gate to the crypt, waiting for the cold-weather night shelter to open. But I am headed half a block farther to the place that is always open to me, because I have the key. I get to go home.

Home. Homeless. Only four letters separate the two, and it sometimes seems much less than that between my clients and me. My colleagues and I are often only a few paychecks or one emergency away from being in the shoes of our clients.

Gillian Hoyer is an Anglican seminarian at Huron University College in London, Ontario. Before moving to London to pursue her education toward ordained ministry, she completed a master's in counseling psychology and worked as a case manager in homeless shelters in Victoria, British Columbia. She blogs sporadically and posts pictures of her adventures on Gillian's Island (gillianhoyer.com)—adventures like having laundry done by the mother of a Papua New Guinean bounty hunter, sipping coffee beside zebras at a Namibian watering hole, and surviving living in a snow belt.

One client tells me of the severe beatings she used to receive at the hands of her mother in the basement of her family home. She has trouble speaking with her mother and is a diligent but troubled mother to her own children when they are not in foster care.

A First Nations client tells me of abuse received at the hands of well-meaning church people who ran the Indian residential school he attended. His culture and language were stripped through beatings and now not only is he between cultures—not identifying with his indigenous heritage and not fitting into dominant white culture—but he can never return to the site of his school in the ancestral home of his people for fear of traumatic flashbacks.

As a Christian, I often hear talk of the tension between the "now" and the "not yet." What I think we're trying to say is that we live in the here and now on earth, but we are looking forward to heaven—that which is to come. It sounds as if we are willing to glide through life here by keeping our eyes fixed ahead on the horizon, avoiding casting our eyes down to the trouble around our feet. "My real home is in heaven," we say, as if to mitigate the cognitive dissonance of these two realities.

If heaven is my real home and it is some place I am longing to get to but have not yet realized, am I actually homeless too? What is earth, if it is not my home? I fear that this language divorces us from the realities of our life on earth. Do we not pray "Thy kingdom come on earth as it is in heaven"?

I am challenged to understand how I can be present in each moment if I am continually looking off to what is to come. This dichotomy of now/not yet presents me with a therapeutic challenge. How can I offer anything to my client, struggling to know how to create a home for her children when she had no safe home life modeled to her, if all I can say is, "Wait for the perfect home in heaven"? How do I attempt any sort of reconciliation with my First Nations client when I, as a member of the church that stripped him of his ability to feel at home in his own skin or on his ancestral land, continue to strip him of that reassurance now by saying, "Don't worry about your identity or home now. Heaven will be worth it"? This seems incredibly disingenuous, coming from someone who has a permanent, warm, dry, comfortable place to live.

But if I am looking for home to be here on earth as it might be in heaven, is being at home simply about having that safe place to hang my hat? What might it be like to put my feet solidly on the earth, look around, and walk a while in the shoes of the people around me?

Home is more than a thing to achieve. It is the people and communities we love, the memories we make together, and the safety and security of a place to rest.

Next time people talk about their home in heaven, I think I might ask them what they are doing to bring that heavenly home to earth. Next time I go to work at the shelter, I want to be mindful of bringing love and a sense of family, safety, and security to everyone I encounter. Because it isn't just the homeless who need a home. We all do.

A Prayer for the Plunger

Rev. Rachel G. Hackenberg

O Holy Wisdom, O Mighty God,
"to whom all hearts are open and from whom no secrets are
    hid,"*
do you know where my sermon is for this week?
Can you help me find the church's toilet plunger?
In your greatness, do you know where
the women's guild hides the good punch bowl and ladle for
    funerals?
Be gracious, O God, and by your mercy
nurture within me a nonanxious spirit
as I navigate all that I do not know.

O Holy Mystery, O Frustrating Wonder,
did you consider the complexity of teaching the Trinity to
    confirmands
when you decided to move in this world as Creator, Christ,
    and Spirit?
As you eavesdrop on the church council's argument over
    new carpet,
do you remember your debate with the Pleiades over the
    color of grass?

Rev. Rachel G. Hackenberg is an author, United Church of Christ minister, and soccer mom. Her books include *Sacred Pause: A Creative Retreat for the Word-Weary Christian* and she blogs at faithandwater.com. She currently serves on the national staff of the United Church of Christ.

Be gracious, O God, and by your mercy
nurture within me a nonanxious spirit
as I navigate all that I do not know.

O Revelatory God, O Discerning Truth,
keep me ever-learning and ever-curious in this ministry,
trusting that there will always be more to know.
Hold me gently when I am overwhelmed.
Let my confidence rest in the eternal faithfulness
    of your love,
and let my uncertainty be lost with the plunger.
Amen.

*Adapted from the Gregorian Sacramentary (seventh century).

The Eruption of Story

Rev. Kerri Parker

The pastor's week is often organized according to the whims of others, the Holy Spirit being among the most frequent offenders.

Once upon a time I envisioned organizing my week around large blocks of time for pondering scripture, writing and editing liturgy, and practicing my sermon in an empty sanctuary. In my head, this was mostly an academic pursuit, and one of the chief claims on a pastor's energy.

God laughs. Large chunks of time for anything are few and far between. There are endless means by which an enterprising pastor can delay the inevitable. Denominational reports and administrative details lurk in the background; parishioners are in need of pastoral care; assorted humanity shows up at the door to help the church spend last Sunday's offering.

The Spirit seems not to be bothered by to-do lists or time lines. This can be counterproductive to good working relationships. If the Divine Person seems not to have a sense of urgency about selecting the week's hymns, the organist and choir director beg to differ. Even so, it pays to wait. The Holy Spirit comes up with much better material than I do alone. I might claim responsibility for a turn of phrase, but she's the one who delivers the gospel door to door.

Rev. Kerri Parker is pastor at McFarland United Church of Christ in McFarland, Wisconsin. In a prior professional life, she was a nonprofit executive and marketing director. She contributed to *Words Matter*, a National Council of Churches (USA) Lenten devotional using expansive language. She blogs at Tell the Stories (tellthestories.blogspot.com). Her favorite means of procrastination are watching *BBC America* with her teenage daughter and finding Christ imagery everywhere.

There's no easy out when you're in the middle of a worship series and writer's block strikes. Having committed to a summer of services informed by musical theater, I was just not feeling that week's show, and *Man of La Mancha* isn't a regular in any lectionary resource I've found to date. It was Wednesday afternoon. I had listened to the sound track so many times that I could sing "The Impossible Dream" in my sleep, and yet the blank screen taunted me. No scripture. No hymns. No prayers. No sermon. Nada.

Then came a knock at the church's front door. I sized up the visitor; his shirt was probably held together by the grease embedded in its fibers, and there wasn't another notch in his belt to be taken in. You might guess he was looking for some help from the pastor's assistance fund, but it always pays to let people tell their own story. At first it was a common tale—living in his van, not interested in going to a shelter, few social connections and fewer social supports.

Then things began to sound very familiar in a different way. He was in the habit of giving his daughter his social security check so she could afford a little place to live. (It's not right for your child to be homeless when you can do something about it, he said.) His other daughter wouldn't talk to him anymore because she disapproved. My oh-so-rational needs assessment came to a grinding halt as I realized he was telling the story of the prodigal family.

When the gospel becomes present tense, you just need to put down your to-do list and your preoccupations and hear it out. Our guest chooses to talk next about the world's sickness. None of it works the way it's supposed to; why do those who have so much choose not to help? He wants to gather twelve people and change things. There have got to be other people, smart like him, who can see that it doesn't have to be this way. Amid the three or four false endings to the conversation, he mentions that he hopes there's a God, and that God is good. In the end, he accepts groceries and a business card, in case he decides he wants to look for a place to sleep that's not a vehicle.

"Don Quixote de la Mancha, the Prodigal Father, and Jesus went into a church ..." It sounds like the beginning of a very bad joke—or perhaps a good one. The Holy Spirit's funny that way. When you let her mess with you, the sacred story infects everything you do and see. You might visit a psychiatric ward that turns out to be the Gerasene tombs after Jesus's unexpected arrival and the pigs' hasty departure. You could be writing an Easter sermon when two women and a child sit down at the foot of the cross in a stripped-bare Good Friday sanctuary, and as you are removed abruptly from your own agenda, your heart is torn as surely as any temple curtain.

There is no telling of the sacred story that does not involve you, and God, and the intersection between the two of you. The Spirit can hold these things together and, on a good day, your soul can too. While time passes and sense escapes at the seams, you will be left with the Holy. A God story will erupt in a quiet building on a day when no one thought much of anything would be going on, and you and the Spirit will have a good laugh.

🍃

Blessed Bedbugs

Rev. Rosalind C. Hughes

I opened the door to find not one but three health inspectors on the step, backed up by the fire chief, just in case. I felt as though I might have hit bottom. I wanted to weep, or at least scream, "*What now?!*" Instead, I invited them in with my best clergy-collared smile.

"We heard about your bedbugs," said one of the health inspectors encouragingly, "so we came to see them."

It was my first solo-clergy gig; I had been at the church for a scant six months. I had found the light switches hidden in fuse box cabinets, learned the trick to opening the columbarium niches in the nick of time, and only locked my keys in the office once (so far). I was doing quite well, until the bedbugs arrived.

It doesn't really matter where they came from; bedbugs, as I was soon to discover, are rampant in our county. Anyone who uses any public space—from the library to the bus, to the doctor's waiting room to the funeral parlor, and even a church—runs the risk of picking up a hidden hitchhiker. Ours had been allowed to take up residence in a rarely entered

Rev. Rosalind C. Hughes is priest in charge at Church of the Epiphany in Euclid, Ohio. Prior to her arrival in Euclid, she had served as curate to Saint Andrew's Episcopal Church, in Elyria, Ohio. Formerly a contributor to *Motherhood Magazine* (Singapore) and *Roots for Churches* (UK), Rosalind maintains a blog of sermons, original poetry, prayers, and other words called Over the Water (rosalindhughes.com). Rosalind moved to the States from her native Great Britain over a decade ago with her husband and their three children; they have since acquired three cats and a rat named Cato.

part of the building, and had taken to heart the biblical imperative to "Go forth and multiply." Hence the interest of the health inspectors.

Officially, bedbugs are not considered a health hazard: they do not spread dirt or disease; they are a simple nuisance. The workers that had first uncovered their hideout, however, had never seen an infestation quite like it, so they told all their colleagues, and now I had city and county personnel on sightseeing tours, lining up outside my door to see the spectacle.

Of course, the officials were barking up the wrong tree. As far as I can tell, if you have seen one bedbug, you've seen them all.

People are something else.

Once the story was out in the open, there was no hiding the little visitors' presence, even though they really did keep to their own corner. Of course, I had to inform my staff and give them the option of staying home until the outbreak was contained. Valiant souls, they stayed. I made awkward phone calls to the various anonymous groups that meet in the evenings; each of them decided that they might just as well risk bedbugs here as at the library.

Not everyone was so unconcerned. First, the preschool closed until assurances could be given that we were not supporting unsolicited biodiversity. Parishioners worried about hosting events two months hence. One even went so far as to suggest canceling Sunday services.

"Do you think anyone will come?" she asked.

"I'll be here," I ventured. In the end, so was she.

In fact, most people rallied quickly. The women's guild chair recounted events held in the company of various species of pests and pestilences in vogue down through the decades—it was practically a tradition, she implied—and the calendar remained unadjusted. Sunday services went off without too much nervous scratching. A generous donor paid the bug-eradication fee, and the preschool rented a sniffer dog, specially trained in bedbug hunting, to make sure that there were no strays left around the building. The director took photos and made a whole presentation to teach the class about bedbugs and sniffer dogs on the children's return.

For a while, I wielded a puppet-master's power, able to make people squirm, fidget, and scratch with a single command word; but it will be a few years before I am ready to make jokes about the bedbugs on Noah's ark from the pulpit.

Yet even bedbugs come with blessings. I bonded with a fellow new-comer over a bonfire in the parking lot, which we tended together, incin-erating infested (and, fortunately, obsolete) paperwork. I finally met the fire chief, and I made friends with a health inspector who turned out to be a handy contact down the road when we wanted to open up our kitchen to cook community meals. I discovered the depth of my leader-ship's commitment to their church and their ability and desire to care for one another and for me. I learned that a preschool teacher will make an object lesson out of practically anything. I realized that opening up, being truthful and trustworthy and honest about our shortcomings as well as our plans to get better, will relieve a multitude of anxieties—our own and those of the community around us. I remembered that God has a pretty expansive sense of humor. Sometimes, the punch line has six legs.

Possessive Voice

Rev. Cheryl Harader

Of all the things I didn't learn in seminary, I think the one that most surprised me was how possessive people are of their pastors. I had heard as a child, and it was reinforced by denominational leadership, that pastors were *called,* not *hired.* But I soon learned the reality that most parishioners think of their pastor as a hired hand, hired to do all the things they don't want to do; paid to be available, at their beck and call.

Don't get me wrong. Being available is one of the most important parts of ministry. Being a nonanxious, faith-filled presence during times of high stress is a vital part of our calling. But sitting in the office, just waiting for someone to drop by and say hi does not fall into the category of "vital" for me.

This expectation confounded me for most of my ministry. Every time I tried to make sense of it, I failed. Other people told me that the requests for me to be in my office so much must be covering up something much deeper. I tried to figure out what that something deeper was. Of course, many people told me that it covered up a desire for a male minister instead

---

Rev. Cheryl Harader is associate pastor of spiritual formation at First Baptist Church in Lawrence, Kansas. She previously served as pastor at First Baptist Church in Winfield, Kansas. She is author of "The Whole Well" and "Discovering Communities" in *Women at the Well: Meditations for Quenching Our Thirst* and blogs at abandonedwaterjars.wordpress.com. She lives with her daughter, Rev. Joanna Harader (also a contributor to *There's a Woman in the Pulpit*), her son-in-law, and three active, fun grandchildren, and has two more grandchildren nearby.

of a female one. *That could explain it*, I thought. I also realized that could take me into dangerous territory. Every complaint I received could fall into the category of "masked desire for a male pastor," which could work well for me. I mean, if the only thing wrong with me is that I'm a woman, and I can't change that, then there's nothing to be done about the complaints except ignore them. Ignoring complaints sounded enticing.

But I just couldn't buy into that.

So I kept trying to guess what the root cause of the complaints might be. What was the true problem? Which of my shortfalls was irritating certain people? And why couldn't they bring themselves to tell me the source of their irritation? Were my sermons too long? Too short? Did I need to preach about hell and Satan? (Well, yes, that had been said.) Did they think my robe was too official for a Baptist church? Did they think I needed to wear a robe all the time, not just occasionally? Did they not like the way I interpreted the Bible? What was really going on?

It didn't take long for this kind of thinking to take over my mind. I wanted to know the *real* reason that I wasn't good enough. It also didn't take long for my focus to turn to the complaints of a few people and away from God. Not a good thing.

And then I had a conversation that changed everything. Well, not *everything*, but it did ease a great deal of my anxiety over this issue.

The chair of the pastor-staff relations board was in my office. We were talking about the new "guidelines" that the board wanted me to follow: (1) be in your office more (no surprise); (2) visit more (*what?*); (3) grow the youth group; and (4) well, to be honest, I've forgotten number 4.

I told the chairperson that I wanted to understand what people thought I should be doing in my office all day. After all, I believe that ministry is in the community—the town and the church community both, but certainly outside the office walls. I told her that the secretary always knew where I was and I would be happy to make appointments at any time. I don't know what else I said, but the chairperson came back with a ... well, it felt like a bomb. It left no doubt in my mind that being in my office *was* the real thing, at least to some people.

The chairperson of the pastor-staff board told me, "We don't care what you do in the office. We just want you in the office. You can paint your toenails if you want."

True story. Sad story. I now understood that my being in the office was extremely important to some people. But I also knew that my being in the office had very little to do with ministry as I understood it. It had little to do with "the priesthood of all believers," and even less to do with serving people, which is our calling.

Paint my toenails? I don't think so.

If you need to find me, ask the secretary. I'll be out in the world, following God's call.

To Laugh at Myself

Rev. Liz Crumlish

"Rosalene would like to meet you and develop a bit of a relationship before she has to plan her funeral" was the request put to me during one of the hospice multidisciplinary team meetings. And so began a brief but intense relationship with a young woman living with a motor neuron disease (ALS). By the time we met, Rosalene was nonverbal. She was, however, in the process of recording her journey, dictating her memoir to her husband by blinking out each letter on a chart. And that was how she communicated with me. She used an early version of predictive text—and sometimes the misinterpretations were hilarious. The tears we shared were more often tears of mirth than sorrow. Although illness was brutally destroying her motor functions, inexorably robbing her of dignity, Rosalene's vibrant spirit and vital sense of humor were not diminished, and visits with her invariably energized me and lifted my spirits.

Rosalene was the first person to christen me "the Vicar of Dibley." She described me in her book as "like the Vicar of Dibley, only younger and slimmer." Little did she know that an ambition of mine was to be able to laugh at myself as well as that BBC character did. In the BBC's *Vicar of Dibley* series, Dawn French plays the village vicar, Geraldine Granger. I've always wanted to mirror her antics—a fun-loving, chocoholic, caring

---

Rev. Liz Crumlish is a Scottish Presbyterian minister living and working on the west coast of Scotland. She has worked as a hospital chaplain and now serves as a parish minister. She loves to spend time walking on the beach, processing thoughts and writing in her head, with the stunning scenery of Scotland as a backdrop.

Anglican vicar, who takes herself and parish life far from seriously and with a huge dose of humor.

A few years later, I was serving in a small village church. Every member of the Vicar of Dibley's parochial board was easily identifiable in the characters who served as officeholders in this parish. There was the inappropriate one who wanted to snog the minister. The one who would arrive late for meetings, smelling of manure or sheep dip. The bumptious one who struggled to serve with a woman vicar. The simplistic and optimistic one, whom everyone merely humored but who often had the best ideas. And the elderly lady whose culinary skills were extremely questionable but who never stopped trying. Board meetings would often disintegrate into heated discussions about milk yields from dairy cattle or about vacuum cleaners or the price of heating oil—almost anything except what was on the agenda. In that parish, some of my most satisfying work was done in the pub when I held out-of-office sessions, arranging weddings and baptisms and, over a good single malt whiskey, becoming embroiled in theological debate or exploring the disciplines of Lent.

The small community, which contained a church, a school, and a pub, grew rapidly as house-building firms discovered its commuter potential. A small shopping development was planned and built, consisting of a grocery store, a pharmacy, and a fast-food restaurant and coffee shop, where we began to host a series of Bible studies.

One memorable day, I walked into the fast-food restaurant and was greeted by the proprietor with "Hi, Geraldine." I accepted this greeting as an accolade.

That Easter, we brought communion onto the streets of our community. With the grand title of "Blood on the Street," we set up a table draped with a white cloth in front of the fast-food place, with the proprietor's blessing, laden with bread and wine. The sign on the table read *It was for you* and as people approached we engaged them in conversation about the symbols of love that we share in the sacrament of communion. The juxtaposition of fast food and soul food really grabbed me. Many of the people who stopped to chat couldn't believe that, though they hadn't set foot in church in years, the sacrament was being offered to them on the streets of their community. Tears flowed as people celebrated the amazing grace of God.

Some might argue that preaching of the word and sacrament must be observed and celebrated together. Others might contend that the sacrament should not be offered to those who have not publicly professed their faith or been baptized, or have not examined themselves in preparation, or numerous other reasons for exclusion. But it was in the places where people gathered outside the church that I discovered the boundless nature of God's grace and was continually reminded that ministry is about being on the streets, sharing the good news, caring through thick and thin, and surviving with a robust sense of humor that mirrors God's tears and belly laughs. It is a ministry fueled by single malt and chocolate and sustained by the deep rumble of laughter that would erupt when the preacher was in danger of taking herself and her faith too seriously.

Don't Call Me "Reverend"

Rev. Denise Anderson

I sit here staring at an electronic copy of my PIF ("Personal Information Form," my denomination's equivalent of a CV or résumé). My general presbyter, who has been wonderfully supportive as I search for my first call, insists I send it to one of the churches in our presbytery. They've been looking for an associate pastor for the past nine months with no success. He thinks I would be perfect for the job, and he's even talked me up to one of the chairs of the nominating committee. What he doesn't know, and what this nominating committee apparently doesn't even remember, is this church had already rejected me—nine months ago.

They're in good company. I've amassed an impressive collection of rejections from churches across the country. It's not unlike when I graduated from college and was looking for my first job. I'm essentially starting a new career, and the hardest part of doing that is getting your foot in the door.

This is my story, this is my song: searching for my first call all the day long.

I've been in the Presbyterian Church for about a decade now, and this denomination's leadership model is simply different from the Baptist and

Rev. Denise Anderson wrote this piece when she was a candidate in the Presbyterian Church (USA). Shortly thereafter, she was called and ordained a teaching elder and can now be called "Reverend." Denise lives in the Washington metropolitan area and is a proud graduate of Howard University School of Divinity. While at Howard, she developed interests in social justice, liberation theology, and feminist/womanist religious thought. She is happily married to the unspeakably awesome Carter and together they have a little girl who aspires to be a shifu in kung fu one day. Denise blogs at soulascriptura.com.

African Methodist Episcopal (AME) churches from which I came. My former churches might have had a number of ordained persons serving at one time, even if only one of them was titled and compensated as the "pastor." In my current tradition, you are ordained to a particular position, so even after earning that MDiv and passing those exams, you are not a "Reverend" until you accept a call from a church or you're called to some other form of recognized ministry. It's always funny to me when my friends in those other denominations ask me, "Girl, why aren't you ordained yet?" They've all been ordained for eons at this point. I finished divinity school six years ago, so to many of my friends and family it seems as if I've been "going into ministry" for forever. They can't comprehend why it would take this long. They aren't the only ones.

Understandably, there are a number of people in my denomination who have the credentials and are certified as ready to receive a call but are not ordained. It's not as if church jobs are in abundance these days. Some have even moved on from their pursuit of ordination and have elected to serve God and humanity in other ways, perhaps as social workers or in the nonprofit sector. I still can't help but feel that God has called me to parish ministry, so my search continues.

I don't mind the wait, however—probably because I stay incredibly busy. For three years, while I progressed through the certification process, I served as the English pastor at a predominantly Asian church. There I was preaching and teaching weekly, doing as much (if not more) than many of my friends in ordained positions. I do pulpit supply at churches. I blog and serve on committees. I attend nearly every stated meeting of our presbytery. Because I feel I'm operating in the call to which God has called me, I don't have a lot of time to lament that I'm not yet ordained. Being in this strange ministerial limbo isn't all that awkward—until someone asks me about it.

I get a lot of requests to preach. I love to preach and I'm always humbled and elated when I'm asked to proclaim the word of our Lord. But that elation is dashed a tiny bit when I receive a draft of the program for the service or event and it reads "Rev. Denise Anderson."

It certainly has a lovely ring to it, and it sure would be nice if it were true. But it's not. What it means is I have to have an uncomfortable conversation with someone's church secretary. I have to break down this convoluted ordination process and explain why, despite how apparently fabulous I am, she can't refer to me as "Reverend." I have to admit that I'm somehow not that credentialed, and maybe even admit that my words and ministry don't have the weight behind them that someone might expect or want them to have. I know I'm projecting my own feelings onto them, and they care much less than I do (if at all). Having these conversations means I'm reminded over and over again of what hasn't happened. And *that* is when it starts to feel weird.

The follow-up question to that conversation is usually this: "Well, what should I call you?"

I don't know—maybe just "Denise"? How about "Ms. Anderson"? For the churches that are big on titles, I can agree to "Minister Anderson." After all, whether we're ordained or not, we're all ministers.

Just don't call me "Reverend"—at least not for now.

I'm Here Because God Cares

Rev. Erin Counihan

As I turned into the parking lot, two men were already running toward me. A third wasn't far behind. I held my breath, offered a quick, "O God, be with me" prayer, and threw the car into park.

I'd been to disaster scenes before. A couple of years riding with sheriffs in Colorado, three years responding to fires and emergencies in Chicago, and two years on the Gulf Coast following Katrina made me, well, not a complete newbie. But I'd never seen anything like this.

It was quieter than I thought it would be. I expected shouting and clapping and sirens and megaphones and the rumble of armored vehicles followed by the crack of rubber bullets being fired. But it was just two o'clock in the afternoon. We who had only seen things on the news didn't know that at 2 p.m. this was just a normal neighborhood.

Except that it was anything but normal. Five days earlier, Michael Brown, an unarmed young black man, had been shot on that street. The one I just drove down. Those men were running to my car from an impromptu aid station that had been set up by neighbors. Residents were walking around, talking, smoking, shaking their heads. Social workers

---

Rev. Erin Counihan is pastor at Oak Hill Presbyterian Church in Saint Louis. She worked eleven years in disaster response and social services before pursuing her call to ministry. When she's not exploring parks with her dog or eating very expensive funnel cakes at free festivals with her niece, Erin occasionally writes about things at somewhatreverend.wordpress.com.

with clipboards, students with posters, community leaders with sweaty stacks of crumpled business cards, and a handful of reporters with their mini steno pads and only slightly larger cameras littered the sidewalk and parking lot. I had just come from a hastily called local clergy gathering where I knew no one, recognized no one (including the U.S. senator and governor who stopped by to address us), to discuss how churches might, or rather should, respond to support the community.

I was three weeks into my very first call, and just three months post seminary graduation, a freshly ordained white girl with New Jersey license plates on my car and a just-bought-at-the-Catholic-supply-store clergy collar, and I was in Ferguson, Missouri.

I missed the class where they teach us how to do this. Maybe I was sick, or at a meeting, or simply did not see the course description in the seminary catalog for "Pastoral Care Under the Influence of Tear Gas." I must have zoned out when the preaching professor reviewed the steps for rewriting a sermon on Sunday morning to address issues like race relations and police brutality on one of your first Sundays in the pulpit before you even have a chance to know who is in the pews—if they're cops, or activists, or people who don't read newspapers.

When you are graduating from seminary, every pastor you meet says, "During your first year in your first call, don't change anything." That's good advice, meant to give you time to listen, observe, and learn on the job. But that good advice goes flying out the window when the community suddenly changes all around you right when you arrive. When there are moms and dads afraid for their kids' lives. When military-grade weapons are thrust in your neighbors' faces. When kids can't go to school because the streets aren't safe. When *discrimination* and *injustice* aren't just words in your sermon, but are painfully seen in the faces of your congregation, your neighborhood, and your city. When you live a mere thirteen miles away and carry a Bible in your purse and have to stand at a microphone in a pulpit every Sunday.

I went to the marches and the protests. I brought my kid. Some church members came too. I met other pastors and business leaders and caseworkers and volunteers and got connected. I learned to drive the neighborhoods and shop, eat, and buy gas at the local stores. I handed out water. I handed out signs. I listened. I stood there and wore my

Catholic-supply-store clergy collar, and I prayed. When I was asked to join a community organizer's work team, I did. When I was asked to question an elected official on next steps, in front of a couple hundred people, I did. When there was nothing to do but sit in my car and scream and cry and pray, I did. When our congregation was asked to house protestors coming in from out of state, we did. We lit candles and discussed and prayed. When we were asked to make donations, we did.

When I drove my Chevy full of baby food and diapers up to the Canfield Apartments for families trapped inside due to curfew and chaos, those three men ran up to me because they hadn't yet seen a white woman come into the neighborhood. They wanted to take pictures with me to show Facebook and Twitter how people of all kinds, from all places, could care about what was happening to them.

"I'm a pastor," I told them, "and I'm here because God cares about you too."

It's Complicated

Being Pastor/Partner/ Parent/Person

So when you see the desolating sacrilege standing in the holy place, as was spoken of by the prophet Daniel (let the reader understand), then those in Judea must flee to the mountains; the one on the housetop must not go down to take what is in the house; someone in the field must not turn back to get a coat. Woe to those who are pregnant and to those who are nursing infants in those days! Pray that your flight may not be in winter or on a sabbath.

MATTHEW 24:15–20

Let the reader understand, on a Sunday morning, when it is time to get to church, we cannot turn back. Whether we live alone in a parsonage fifty feet from the sanctuary or ten minutes away with a spouse to mind our children, or an hour's country ride with peace to practice our sermon, there comes a moment when we cannot turn back. Our time is God's, and our effort must focus on the people in front of us, even though the other people and pets and worries and responsibilities that come with being alive remain in the back of our mind.

In the words of everyone's favorite Facebook relationship description: It's complicated.

Unlike other professional women, we live with the expectation that we will reveal ourselves to people who are both our employers and the recipients of our care, teaching, and spiritual leadership. They know our son has a peanut allergy because they feed him snacks after church. They know our daughter has a boyfriend because he showed up at the late service on Christmas Eve. They try to set us up on unwanted dates, or they suspect something is off in our marriage because they haven't seen our spouse lately. They needed to call us as a part-time pastor, but worry that our other job will get in the way of ministry.

It's complicated.

The details of our lives are open for examination. We have been the forty-something mother of teenagers asked how strongly she feels about including the denomination's maternity leave policy in her call agreement. ("I hope we don't have to find out?") We have been the single woman who learns of an anonymous letter asking, "Is it true there are two lesbians living in the manse?" ("Not yet, but someday, one hopes.") We have been the mom whose kid comes to church in his soccer cleats, or even the preacher who tries to get the communion service done in its appointed hour because under her robe there are softball togs. (No one minds when church ends on time.)

Let the reader understand, it's complicated, having more than one hat (or ball cap) to wear. But woe to those who think we can't manage it, because we can. (Most of the time.)

Always the Pastor, Never the Bride

Rev. Michelle L. Torigian

... do not stir up or awaken love until it is ready!
SONG OF SOLOMON 3:5

The wedding begins at five o'clock. I prepare by adorning my hair with spiral curls and clothing myself in flowing white garments for the ceremony. The vows are on the tip of my tongue.

But the attire isn't a wedding dress; it's a robe. And the self-curled tresses are the elegant style of yours truly, the pastor solemnizing the marriage.

I'm always the pastor and never the bride ...

I find that each time a new couple calls for my services, I get a strange little feeling in the pit of my stomach. Nowadays, at forty-one, I'm practically old enough to be the mother of the bride. And yet I've never been a bride myself.

Rev. Michelle L. Torigian is pastor of Saint Paul United Church of Christ in Cincinnati. This is her first call in ministry, before which she worked in fund-raising and marketing for nonprofits. She is the author of many articles on the *Huffington Post* religion page, including "Between Childless and Childfree," a reflection for Mother's Day. She regularly posts her musings on current events, pop culture, and theology at michelletorigian.com. To help capture God's presence in the small moments in life, she pulls out her phone and instagrams the unique view in front of her.

Admittedly, there have been pangs of jealousy through which I've had to work. Over the years there have been a plentitude of conversations between God and me. Wondering if I will ever have this opportunity in my personal life, I've ridden the roller coaster of emotions. *Seriously God—why not me? Why were they able to find each other? God, I'm being patient here ... When will it be my turn?*

I never get a direct answer, just a request from another engaged couple wanting my services.

There have been times that this has been one of the most challenging parts of my call to ministry. I don't mean performing the ceremony itself or even talking with the couple. What is challenging is realizing that feelings often pop up during the course of our conversations. I remember the hope lost as a long-term relationship ended. My idea of love went from being this idealized dream state when I was in my twenties to something more concrete, cherished, and sacred in my forties. No longer is the hoped-for wedding day a "fairy tale come true" but the threshold to the next phase of life's peaks and valleys, journeying with the one I love.

In preparation for a wedding, I schedule three or four sessions with the couple, realizing that through these sessions, we all have a chance to better know one another before the ceremony. We talk through the details of the wedding, and I stress to them the importance of tailoring the service to their uniqueness as a couple. During our meetings, I lead them through a workbook of questions that requires them to talk with each other. I add some questions that spark conversations on how they chose each other, why they desire marriage, how their family structures have impacted who they are today, and how they have strengthened each other's lives. I ask myself, *If I were entering this type of commitment, what would I want to speak about with my betrothed in the preparation process?*

Some would say that I'm not qualified to lead a couple through premarital pastoral care sessions because I've never been married. Like any other clergyperson, I can't tell them if they're ready to get married or not—that's between them and God. I can't guarantee them a successful marriage; marriages evolve over the years, and how they react and communicate will be their key to success. As long as there is no abuse and each of them is willing to listen to their beloved, any couple has a chance of success. By having these sessions with them, I know they are talking through issues, and I pray that this will encourage healthy communication between these two who are committing their lives to each other.

No matter whose marriage I am solemnizing, I learn something about love, communication, and commitment. By walking with others through their preparation process, I have realized that the level of love we are aiming for is one that reflects the love of God. We read in 1 Corinthians 13:12, "For now we see in a mirror, dimly, but then we shall see face to face. Now I know only in part; then I will know fully, even as I have been fully known." Only God sees us for who we truly are. Knowing that our spouse will never fully understand us as God does, we must allow for grace in the relationship. Likewise, we are called to do our best at viewing our loved ones as God views us: beautifully broken, messy children of God who are also made in God's image.

It's taken a while for love to stir in my life. I'm not like some people who began dating in their teens or twenties. By being a pastor before hopefully someday becoming a bride, I've come to appreciate the heart of a wedding day: the unique commitment between two hope-filled people and the promise to look at our loved ones through the eyes of God. I hold on to that hope as I embrace the love to which God is calling me.

Preaching Ahead of Yourself

Rev. Robin Craig

How will I ever preach a sermon again? The question arose about five months after my son died by suicide.

I had preached only a very few sermons, in my home church and as a guest elsewhere, but I had *heard* hundreds of them, and the combined experience of speaking and listening had helped to propel me into seminary as a midlife student. The first year had gone well, but the second had not gone at all.

My son died the week before classes commenced in the fall, and I didn't return to seminary until the winter quarter began in December.

Stunned, shocked, drenched in a grief that had rendered me all but incapacitated, I wondered all fall whether to return to school. "Mom," my daughter said, calling from her distant college, "you have to get out of bed."

"Lord," said Peter, in words spoken two thousand years ago, "to whom can we go?"

Rev. Robin Craig is pastor of Boulevard Presbyterian Church in Euclid, Ohio, having previously served as pastor of Nankin Federated Church in Nankin, Ohio. She is also a spiritual director and retreat leader trained in the Ignatian tradition. Her article "Ignatian Spirituality: Companionship in Loss" appeared in *Presence*, the journal of Spiritual Directors International. She blogs at metanoia-mrc. blogspot.com. Robin and her husband are the parents of three children, and are trying to figure out how to move gracefully into the third third of life.

"I think," said my spiritual director, sitting with me in a parlor darkened by the winter as well as by my own blackened heart, "that you should try, if you can."

God, as far as I could tell, had departed the universe. But I returned to seminary anyway, where I bumped up against homiletics, a required class unexpectedly moved to the spring quarter. I would not have gone back had I known it was coming up so fast.

I met with the professor to learn what would be expected of me. Reading, writing, remembering, speaking—clearly nothing that I could hope to accomplish. I debated what to do as I stood in the cafeteria line with classmates one day. A friend remarked, "You will be studying and preaching the gospel—what could be more healing than that?"

There is no healing to be had, I thought. I signed up for the course anyway.

In class, I preached on the Twenty-Third Psalm. I despised the Twenty-Third Psalm. I had completed my required unit of clinical pastoral education the summer before my son died, and I had prayed the Twenty-Third Psalm with dozens of dying patients and their families. I hoped never to hear it again. But there it was, an assigned text, so I preached it.

I preached about the tables set for us by beloved friends in the presence of the enemies that we call death and bewilderment and anguish. Words formed themselves independent of my grief. I preached about how God sets tables for us even in the absence of all for which and for whom we long.

"You have a communion sermon," offered one of my classmates.

Really? A sermon? Words beyond a descent into the hopelessness and despair that I felt? Something that might be termed good news?

Perhaps, I considered, it is possible to preach ahead of yourself. Ahead of your wobbly, unconvinced, heartbroken self.

That became my motto: Preach ahead of yourself. Preach what you hope to know again one day. Preach the confidence for which you long. Preach the promises awaiting fulfillment. Preach the peace that seems utterly elusive. Preach the practices you follow, despite the bone-dry life on which they leave no imprint.

Preachers have been preaching ahead of themselves for centuries. Pastors step into the pulpit notwithstanding the divorce papers on the desk, the child in the hospital, the mother's funeral the next day.

Some of these pastors are able to preach the goodness of God because they rest in the assurance of God's love, despite the outward circumstances of their lives. Others of us preach the abundant love of God from the center of a bleak and frigid landscape in which the sound of God is the sound of silence.

How? We can do it only because the Christian faith is rooted in hope, a hope so strong that it prevails even when we on our own cannot, a hope that promises wholeness.

Some months ago I went on a silent retreat, during which I wondered, *What is it about Jesus that is so compelling?* Jesus, I saw, is wholeness. The one completely broken before our eyes is the only completely whole person in the narrative of human history. And Jesus offers to us his presence that we might eat and drink of complete love and ourselves become whole.

Jesus reshapes even the broken body of a beloved child into wholeness healed and reclaimed by love.

And so, I hope. I still preach ahead of myself. It's not a matter about which I am explicit from the pulpit, but it seems to me that people hear in my words a longing that echoes theirs, and a confirmation that our longings will be fulfilled. Perhaps that is gift enough for someone called to share good news.

How Does *That* Work?

Rev. Beth Birkholz

It's the first question I get when I tell someone that I'm a pastor, and my husband is a pastor too, but at a different church. (And we have *kids*!)

They tilt their heads as if to see me better, and ask that question: "How does *that* work?" It's as if we had done some crazy feat of acro-yoga, ending up with a double twist dismount, instead of just going to our jobs and raising our kids like people do every day.

Well, my house may be the rare place where you'd hear either partner say, "Did you take my #$%^ home communion kit?" or "How could you have used *all* my clerical collar tabs??" (Answers: "No, it's in your trunk"; and "Sorry!" Now I wear a Roman collar instead of tabs so I can find them more easily.) But that doesn't mean that we're total weirdos. We have crazy-busy lives, full of sports and children and lately a minivan (horrors!), plus dogs, cats, and chickens, which means, basically, we're a family from the suburbs who just happens to work for Jesus.

I could not have predicted this when my husband-to-be, Scott, offered me a beer in the seminary courtyard, right before our Greek class started for the summer. One time that summer we led worship together, and it was super cool in the way that only baby pastors (twenty-two! so young!), trying to stir up some controversy, can understand. As far as I can remember, in the seventeen years since, that has never happened again.

Rev. Beth Birkholz is associate pastor at Holy Trinity Lutheran Church in Marietta, Georgia. Formerly she served at two smaller churches in the mountains of Georgia and one larger one in downtown Atlanta. She blogs at chickpastor.wordpress.com, and would like to be on the lake on her paddleboard right this minute.

This is just fine with us, for the most part. On the rare occasion that we do sit together in worship, such as during another pastor's installation or our church assembly, we behave *terribly*. We giggle. We pass notes. It's kind of ridiculous, because it's such a novelty. It's a little shocking that we're always asked if we want to work together, even by our governing body, each and every time one of us is eligible for call. But when it gets down to it, it's a rare person who can have the same life partner as work partner and have it work out well. We're okay with this; it's the rest of the world that seems to have a bit of an issue.

The rest of the world also *really* wants to know what we do on Sunday mornings with our beloved children. When I look back on it, a Sunday nanny would have been a *fantastic* idea, but most of the time our salaries wouldn't allow for that kind of luxury. During what I call the "dark times," the kids came with me because I had a small mission church with one service. Also, the whole breast-feeding situation made it difficult to pawn them off on Dad for the six hours that was his busy Sunday at a larger church. As it was, I'd be preaching and hear my daughter crying in the nursery during the only hour she was away from me that week. She was held by loving nursery attendants, God bless them, but in those years I would have loved to have an additional parent there, rather than depending on one hour of child care, a baby sling, and a consignment-sale baby bouncer. How did that work? Not great.

The thing about kids, though, is that they grow up. As they got older, my husband moved to a smaller church and I went to a bigger one. Then they went with him almost every time, and he became the one who was stressed by Sunday worship prep, with kiddos tagging along. I got to "luxuriate" at my larger church alone (with my own bathroom!), but I missed them coming with me.

Our lives have just started to be complicated with things like friends and youth group for our kids, but we're at much happier places, emotionally and physically. The kids decide where they go each Sunday (the night before, please, as well as picking out their outfits) with full disclosure from us about how many meetings they'll be sitting through and when we can leave and get to Five Guys for lunch.

How does that work? Pretty damn well, actually.

My favorite author, Anne Lamott, says that one of the most subversive things you can do is show up for your life and not be ashamed.* No matter what, no matter how strange our family seems or how much we get that weird look, we try our best to be grateful to God for our odd blessings, to love each other, to show up for our lives, and not to be ashamed.

---

* Anne Lamott, *Operating Instructions: A Journal of My Son's First Year* (New York: Anchor Books, 1993), 100.

I Rise Before the Sun

Rev. Stacey Simpson Duke

I rise before the sun does, to sit in silence with coffee and cat, so I can create things out of yarn. I learned to knit from a book, on a whim, not long after I moved from Georgia to Michigan, thinking it would be a nice diversion during long, cold months of being cooped up inside. Knitting has turned out to be not so much a diversion as a portal—a doorway to a deeper connection with my truest self, an entrance into a new kind of community with others, and an opening into a fresh sense of companionship with our collaborative, creative God.

In those early days, I couldn't quite get over the magical nature of this ancient craft: Through the simple act of patiently, persistently, precisely pulling loop through loop, the knitter creates something that wasn't there before. With only basic raw materials and the simplest of hand movements, whole new creations come into being. All these years later, I'm still enchanted by the process and its surprising outcomes—all I have to do is just persist, stitch by stitch, and one day something beautiful will emerge.

As a pastor, most of my vocational life revolves around things that can't be seen—words, ideas, relationships, values (not to mention God!). The fact that none of these things can be seen doesn't make them unreal,

---

Rev. Stacey Simpson Duke is co-pastor of First Baptist Church of Ann Arbor, Michigan, along with her husband, Paul, with whom she also shares the role of campus minister of the American Baptist Campus Foundation at the University of Michigan. She is author most recently of three articles in *Feasting on the Gospels: Matthew*. In her spare time, she knits, spins wool, weaves, sews, and enjoys being mother to her twin ten-year-old sons. She blogs at earthchicknits.com.

but it does make them hard to measure, which can be daunting. At the end of any given week of work, I look back and sometimes wonder what I have to show for all my hours. To produce something with my own hands, something that can be seen and touched by anyone, has had a profound, anchoring effect on me. To start the day with something as physical and elemental as making something with my hands not only helps locate me in my body, it helps me recognize again my kinship with a God who creates. And as sheep's wool slides through my fingers and wooden needles click in my hands, I feel connected to the earth, and to the animals, and to every person who has ever put sticks and strings together in hopes of making something lovely and warm. Knitting knits me together.

So every day I spend a little time alone, doing something that does not depend on intelligence, eloquence, charisma, or pastoral sensitivity; it just depends on showing up. It never demands more than I can do or give, because it isn't something I do in response to anyone else's expectations. If I make a mistake, I can undo it and make things exactly right, or I can accept it and learn to live with the imperfection. Because I always have this choice, mistakes have lost their power. Knitting teaches me every day about prayer and grace and patience and gentleness.

There have been times I have felt the need to justify my craft, as if a professional woman juggling the demands of leading a church and raising young children shouldn't spend time on something so nonessential as making pretty things. Other times, I have felt pressure to do something ministry-related with my hobby, like making prayer shawls for the ill or hats for the homeless. For me, however, knitting has become its own justification, a challenge to the idea that everything I do has to be important or useful or in service to others. When I get up early and knit, it is a way of reminding myself that I am free, that there is space in my life for all of me, and not just the "minister" me or the "mom" me; that there is room in my life to do some things simply because I enjoy them. Knitting is a valuable practice on its own terms, which reminds me that I am a valuable person on my own terms, and not just because I do valuable things.

Knitting wakes me up, and more than just physically. It wakes me up daily and deeply to the stunning, God-given reality of who I really am—someone made in the image of the Creator and who, therefore, can create, with freedom and with joy. And so I rise.

Out Standing in Her Field
A Pastoral (De)Composition

Rev. Holly S. Morrison

Saint Brigid's Day, an hour before dawn

She is my favorite Celtic saint, Brigid: patron of midwives, lactating animals, chicken farmers, blacksmiths, and poets. A cold sliver of moon was caught in the rosy sky above ground frozen hard as stone. As my wife headed outside to check our Highland cattle, I opened the woodstove to feed the fire, then put on a kettle—not for tea, but for pouring hot water onto the rims of the frozen water dispensers in the henhouse. I was warmed by more than the stove: in an hour or two, I'd begin a long-awaited stint of mentored service at a local church. I heard a strange sound from the pasture and ran to the window to look. There, at the edge of the pasture, stood my wife and fellow farmer, her face twisted with shock. Beyond her, on a snowy slope, our best-bred heifer lay on her side, her legs jutting out stiff and straight from her body.

Rev. Holly S. Morrison is pastor at Poland Community Church (UCC) in Poland, Maine, and previously served United Methodist and Mennonite congregations in Alaska, Colorado, and Washington state. She is the prizewinning author of "Screevins frae a Bothy in Maine" in *The Smeddum Test: 21st-Century Poems in Scots*. She blogs at mainecowgaels.blogspot.com. She feeds her fires with shared songs, organic farm goods, wild late-night board games, and her wife's banjo and bagpipe tunes. They share the farm with assorted farmhands and a somewhat judgmental border collie.

The sun began to rise, slowly illuminating our tableau of confused grief. There was no rhyme or reason to this death, no obvious illness or accident, only the sharp irony of losing a pregnant heifer on the feast day of a dairy saint. I kneeled, stroking the heifer's smooth horns and thick brown coat. I said a prayer for all she had given us, for the hopes and possibilities she'd carried. Then there were logistics to sort out. I put my grief on hold. There was no chance of burial with the ground this hard. I called other farmers to see what we should do. When the hour was late enough for nonfarm folk to be stirring, I called the senior pastor of the church. "I'm sorry—I know it's my first day—but I'm going to be late. I have to compost a cow."

I'm a farmer and a pastor. Both aspects of my life are shaped by the traditions of my Welsh and Scottish ancestors, whose double bonds to cattle and Christianity reach back into the mists of time. I am convinced of the sacredness of all creation and tend my farm accordingly. I believe, with Wendell Berry and other agrarians, in the redemptive power of compost. But I never thought I'd have to compost a cow. Still, it was the only safe way to deal with her body. On the counsel of elder farmers, confirmed by a state farm advisor, we spent the morning preparing a very large, very hot compost pile—a sort of slow-burning funeral pyre. A neighbor with a tractor helped maneuver the large carcass into its midst and blanketed her body with a final thick layer of used horse bedding. The steam began to rise almost immediately. I went inside, threw another log in the woodstove, changed my clothes, and went to work.

I didn't expect it to be such an icebreaker, but everyone at that rural church loved the story. One older man—still sporting a ponytail and the occasional paisley shirt—declared gleefully that, when his time came, he wanted to be composted too! While I inwardly vowed that I would never let farming interfere with church again, members of the congregation pressed me for farm news constantly. Livestock and orchards made their way into my sermons, and I laughed when my assigned preaching days, often as not, featured agriculture in the lectionary.

Other church connections and duties came my way. I served on denominational committees and commissions, gradually absorbing the lingo and idioms. I learned to code-switch from the picturesque yet blunt talk of farmers to the nuanced "soft verbs" of the United Church of Christ.

My clergy mentor seemed to sense my challenges implicitly. Though she could play the cello, preach a riveting sermon, and run a tight congregational meeting with the best of them, she too had grown up in farm country. Still, it wasn't until my very last day on the job that I knew just *how* thoroughly she understood.

It was my final Sunday. I was about to deliver my last benediction, when the pastor went to the pulpit. "Hold on a minute, Holly," she announced. "We're not quite through with you yet." She reached behind a partition and pulled out a bewilderingly bulky ... *something*, draped in fabric. "We wanted to give you a useful gift for the years ahead, something you can use in both your vocations." She reminded the congregation of the phone call she'd received from me on my first day of work. Then, with a glint in her eye, she handed me the cloth-draped object, whispering, "I was up late last night, embellishing." I pulled off the fabric to find a sturdy tool of iron and wood, bedecked with a hand-carved denominational symbol: my very own UCC manure fork.

Why Is My Pillow Hot?
A Prayer

Rev. Julia Seymour

O God.

Why is my pillow hot, my chair hard, my soup cold, my coffee skinned?

I toss and I turn, with too many things on my mind.

I'm tired of sitting, of forms, papers, books, spread far and wide.

I took a phone call, hurried to meet someone—lunch forgotten.

I poured the cup, started listening, and never drank.

The questions have answers, but they still keep coming.

Is this my life or Your Life disguised as mine?

I remember that I am *not* you.

Question: Do you remember?

What is truth? Where are you going? Who will save us?

Spirit of water and air, I have lost track of where you begin and I end.

The problem is, I seem to do that with everyone.

Rev. Julia Seymour has been the ordained minister at Lutheran Church of Hope in Anchorage, Alaska, since August 2008. She believes strongly in ecumenical and interfaith cooperation. She blogs at lutheranjulia.blogspot.com. Julia enjoys reading, writing, crochet, and outdoor activities. She lives with her husband, their two young children, and their devoted Labrador retriever.

Children, parents, spouse, partner, friends, parishioners,
    strangers—
The connections are intense, profound, meaningful.
They are too close, too painful, too much.
I see you in them, even though I may not be revealing your
    glory at the moment.
This is the work to which you have called me.
This is the joy, which you have revealed to me.
These are the depths I do not plumb alone.
These are the paths I trip over, to be caught by you.
Ravel me in and knit me into your kin-dom, in its perfect
    shape and drape,
So that I can be the stripe that completes your work—where
    you have placed me.
The pillow has a cool side. A cushion is found. The soup
    reheats. A new cup is poured.
And still your grace is more than enough for all I will ever
    need.
Amen.

A Vegetarian in the Church

Rev. Teri Peterson

As a kid, I never gave up trying to hide food I didn't like. It never worked. After one meal where I left the table several times, my mother started asking to see inside my mouth before I went. I didn't love all my veggies, but it was bites of steak and meat loaf that found their way into my napkin and down the drain. Growing up on a farm, that was confusing as all get-out to everyone else. It still is. I've been a vegetarian for sixteen years now and my grandmother still insists, "But you used to eat it and like it!"

My grandparents aren't the only ones who are confused. The church world is surprisingly meat-centric for a community gathered around bread and wine. It is also rarely veggie-friendly, though vegetarianism has moved into the mainstream. The word *potluck* evokes visions of broccoli-bacon salad, sausage casseroles, and Jell-O "salads." The rise of the organic movement, Whole Foods, and kale chips have brought plant-based diets into our collective cultural consciousness. But at the individual level, and the congregational level, being vegetarian is still viewed as a little weird, and possibly suspicious.

As a vegetarian pastor, I want to be careful not to make things all about me, while also not skipping the spread at a church dinner. I have learned to

---

Rev. Teri Peterson is pastor at the Presbyterian Church of Palatine, Illinois. She previously served six years as associate pastor at the Ridgefield–Crystal Lake Presbyterian Church. She and her best friend Amy Fetterman coauthored *Who's Got Time? Spirituality for a Busy Generation* and regularly present workshops on that theme. Teri has blogged for more than a decade at CleverTitleHere (clevertitlehere.blogspot.com). She lives a typical suburban life, filled with cat purrs, *Doctor Who*, and commuting.

always bring two dishes to a potluck, so it will look like I'm eating plenty. I have practiced my mother's advice about accepting dinner invitations since she first offered it sixteen years ago: "Always say, 'Yes, thank you! I would love to come to dinner. I'm a vegetarian, so would you like me to bring something?'" Sometimes I add that my favorite foods are all side dishes, so no matter what they prepare, I'm likely to be perfectly happy. When it comes to announcements, I am often publicly self-deprecating about being a vegetarian. Still, my dietary choices inevitably spark curiosity.

These conversations usually begin with "I don't really know how to cook vegetarian." This is almost always an apology for something amazingly delicious. It is also almost always a precursor to the real question: "So why are you a vegetarian, anyway?"

I have answered this question in homes and restaurants, in church fellowship halls and around the grill at the picnic. I have given answers to teenagers who want to know "If someone held a gun to your head and told you to eat a hamburger, would you do it?" and to people living with homelessness and eating dinner in our church basement.

It's that last one that is the hardest, of course. My reasons for being a vegetarian are a complicated mix of environmentalism, animal rights, human rights, social justice, economic reality, and personal taste. I usually say that there is so much violence inherent in the production of meat, and I choose not to ingest violence in that way. And yet I recognize that a statement like that can sound judgmental—do I think other people are eating violence and "you are what you eat"? It also sounds like a reflection of incredible privilege to someone who only gets one meal a day, and that meal is whatever the volunteers are serving.

It is a privilege to be able to choose what I eat. I try to use that privilege to support local farmers, to share plant-based recipes with people who still believe vegetarians subsist on nothing but salad, and to be the kind of vegetarian who isn't judgmental. If I am going to say that part of my reasoning is that I do not want to participate in this particular system of violence, then I have to be ready to actually not participate in the system of violence ... with my words and actions, not just my fork. I hope that vegetarianism is fuel for my commitment to being a peacemaker in the world.

Jesus calls us to be makers of peace, creators of justice. In the body of Christ, many go hungry and thirsty, in part because of our culture's systems of food production, distribution, and consumption. Being mindful of what we eat ought to be a part of our calling as a body, just as we are mindful of how we spend our time and our money. I don't believe it is my place to prescribe anyone else's food choices. I do believe that food is central to our Christian faith, and that being a vegetarian is part of my witness and part of my calling. It isn't just a dietary choice; it's part of my identity—I am a child of God, I am a pastor, I am a vegetarian. These pieces of my identity inform all my choices, every day—from where I shop to what I wear to how I interact with the people around me.

So invite me to your potluck—I'll bring at least two things, they'll be delicious, and they won't be salad.

Uncloseted

Rev. Patricia J. Raube

Memory is a funny thing. When I think back on the months that led up to my coming out of the closet to my congregation, memory constructs a fairly linear process.

First, I decided to read and blog the daily lectionary passages as my Lenten spiritual discipline.

Next, I read the epistle for Ash Wednesday: 2 Corinthians 5:20–6:10, which reads, in part:

> For [God] says, "At an acceptable time I have listened to you, and on a day of salvation I have helped you." See, now is the acceptable time; see, now is the day of salvation!

And then, inspired by Paul's words, and bolstered by the support of family and friends, I decided to come out! Cue the confetti and streamers.

But I have a blog—mostly an archive now, as I have written less and less about being a "closeted pastor" since I stopped being one. And that blog tells a slightly different story.

Rev. Patricia J. Raube is pastor of Union Presbyterian Church in Endicott, New York. Prior to that she served in several interim positions, including that of interim chaplain of the Protestant Cooperative Ministry at Cornell University. She wrote "Blessed Is She Who Believes" for *Daughters of Sarah: The Magazine for Christian Feminists*. She blogs her sermons at upcsermonsandmore.blogspot.com and maintains an archive at ceciliainthecloset.blogspot.com. Her children, Ned and Joan, are finding their way as actors and artists, and her partner, Sher, continues to listen carefully, and always, always, speaks the truth in love.

Almost a month before Lent begins, I find an entry titled, "On Clos-etedness, and the Choosing of It." In that piece I explain that, when I was ordained, I was in a heterosexual marriage that I fully expected to be life-long. My expectations were wrong. And when—to my delight!—I found true love with a woman, I really had no choice (or so I thought). I had to be closeted, I told myself, if I wanted to continue to serve the church as a minister.

A week later, in a post on the film *Milk*, I wrote:

> As he gains more prominence ... Harvey seems to know he is likely to be assassinated.... He understands the likely cost of his activism.... [He] says, "If a bullet should enter my brain, let that bullet destroy every closet door."

Cue me, weeping, in the darkened theater, clenching my beloved's hand.

Two days before Ash Wednesday, there's a post titled "Secrets." Here I try to make a case that being closeted isn't about secrecy, it's about *privacy*.

And then someone I'd never met, but who I had come to know in that most intimate and virtual of ways, called me out. "August" told me that it was all very well and good to speak of privacy and boundaries, but in her mind, the only two possible *excuses* for remaining in the closet were either shame or self-interest. Self-interest, to an extent, she understood. But, she wrote,

> If shame is the real reason you are closeted, [it does] a huge disservice to the people you serve.... Imagine—you have a gay parishioner struggling with her identity, and she becomes aware somehow that the preacher she respects and trusts is "hiding" the fact of her own lesbianism.... It would shatter any trust she might have had with her minister, and—worse—reinforce her own hunch that God, after all, does not love her as she is.

Cue me, mentally going through the church directory, wondering whether I had already done damage ... And it dawned on me that the children were watching—my own children and the children of the congregation.

On the second day of Lent I drove my daughter, Joan, to her voice lesson. She was a sophomore in high school, and happily active in my— *our*—congregation. I said, "Don't be anxious ... I'm thinking of coming out to the congregation. And, you know—it might result in my having to leave the church. I'm not sure what the outcome would be. What do you think?"

I was driving up a long suburban hill in the February twilight. My heart was in my mouth.

She spoke very carefully. "I think it would be a really good idea," she said. "The people at church love you. I think most of them would be fine. And even if you ended up needing to leave, I think it's always a better idea to be honest about who you are." It was decided.

Later that night I spoke to my beloved on the phone. She listened quietly. She had been out for many years, but she knew—she had *lived*—both sides of this story. Finally, she spoke.

"I think it's always a bigger deal inside your own head than it is to the rest of the world. After years of being closeted at work, I found out, when I came out, that they already knew, and mostly didn't care."

I wondered whether my congregation, the people I loved, would care. I learned that they did—in marvelous ways. When I came out a few months later, they flooded me with supportive phone calls and emails. They said things like, "We're so happy you are in a relationship that makes you happy!" They asked whether my partner might like to *sing in the choir*. Even those who had concerns about what scripture might have to say welcomed me into their homes, let me pray with them, and told me they loved me, that I was their pastor.

Memory is a funny thing. The specifics of my story are made clear in the digital record, blog post after blog post, and those specifics don't always line up with the narrative as my memory preserved it. But how the welcoming, loving people of God made me feel is forever set as a seal upon my heart.

I Pray with My Eyes Open

Rev. Mindi Welton-Mitchell

When I began professional ministry as a young single minister, on Sunday mornings all I needed were my keys, my wallet, and my Bible. Flashforward six years, and I was packing a bag with diapers, wipes, bottles, a change of clothes for my baby, and an extra blouse in case I was spit up on.

I never imagined that twelve years later I would live next door to the church yet still be packing a diaper bag, a lunch, and an iPad to take with me on Sunday mornings. My son has autism, and uses the iPad for communication.

We walk to my office, twenty feet from the parsonage, at 9:15. My son turns on all the lights in the office and immediately goes to the toy box, usually dumping it upside down. During Sunday school, I lead Bible study for adults while he plays at our feet, occasionally interrupting me on his iPad to tell me he is ready for his snack.

Following Sunday school, we walk to the church building together. I sit my son down on the front pew at 10:45 and open his lunch because he is used to eating lunch at eleven o'clock every day, and, of course, worship

---

Rev. Mindi Welton-Mitchell is currently pastor of Burien Community Church (American Baptist) in Burien, Washington, and is also on staff at Open Gathering Christian Church, a Disciples of Christ new church plant. She previously was senior pastor of First Baptist Church in Framingham, Massachusetts. She wrote a chapter in *The Modern Magnificat: Women Responding to the Call of God*, edited by fellow RevGal Jennifer Harris Dault, and writes weekly worship resources at Rev-o-lution (rev-o-lution.org). She is married to Rev. J. C. Mitchell and is the mother of A. J., who has autism.

begins at eleven. While I greet people as they arrive, my son often runs up and down the aisle more than once before I am able to corral him and locate him in the front pew again.

I have led worship while my son began to have a meltdown. I have prayed with my eyes open, watching my son crawl under the pews. I have announced to the congregation, "Please be seated," and immediately added, in a louder, sharper voice, "A. J., sit down!" as he stands on his tip-toes on the edge of a pew. I have led worship on two hours of sleep when A. J. has struggled to sleep through the night. I have to trust the Holy Spirit to carry me through on the difficult days.

This is Sunday morning for a pastor and a mom of a child with autism. I am half of a clergy couple, but my husband commutes a half hour on Sunday mornings to another town, and going along would add an extra hour to my son's already long Sunday schedule. Most Sundays he comes with me. It has taken time for the congregation to get used to him. At first, many found him loud and distracting. Even though they were introduced to him during the search process, even though I wrote a letter to the congregation about him, they still did not understand until they experienced him in worship.

The main difficulty of being a clergy mom of a child with a disability is that people are afraid to help. They are afraid they don't know what to do and don't know enough. When my son was a baby, before we had any cause for concern, I never ran out of volunteers willing to hold him or care for him. That all changed once we had a diagnosis of autism. It took a long time before people in my current congregation felt comfortable enough to respond to my requests for help.

Now A. J. is part of the congregation and no one is distracted by his behavior anymore. Everyone greets him and offers him a high-five or a hug. They smile when they see him run up and down the aisle—which has become rarer as he matures and becomes used to the Sunday routine. I have volunteers in the church who, after the greeting time, will take A. J. to the back pew, where he can lie down or move around without disturbing too many people or distracting me. He is welcomed with open arms at children's church, where he can stack blocks or write letters, or at times simply run back and forth to get his energy out. He loves coffee hour—and who wouldn't, when it is the one hour of the week that I do not care how many cookies he has? People are excited when they experience the developmental milestones he has made, when he smiles, when he says hi, and when he gives hugs.

Our congregation has grown in our understanding of welcoming and accepting people of all abilities. We recently received a grant to hold an inclusive day camp for children with disabilities and their typically developing peers.

For me, my identities as pastor and mom are intertwined. As A. J.'s mom, I am constantly advocating for him, whether it is to be included in activities typically developing children are included in, or in school, to have the best resources available for him to grow. It is no different in the church. Every Sunday, I am advocating for my son to be included as a child of God in the church. Every Sunday, I pray with my eyes open.

The Parson

Rev. Katherine Willis Pershey

Sometimes I don't know when I'm working and when I'm not. I read biblical commentaries while I nurse my daughter. I engage in personal prayer as I prepare to lead corporate worship. I facilitate a small group at church for young mothers, and if you eavesdropped on that group you might not guess that I'm the young mother who also happens to be one of the associate pastors. I wrote a spiritual memoir about my personal life that has opened countless doorways for pastoral care.

Everyone ponders work while they wash the dishes (at least I presume they do). Some professions are fairly easy to walk away from at five o'clock; leadership positions such as pastoral ministry are not. But it's not just my work bleeding into my life; it's vice versa. My family is deeply involved with my congregation. My husband (a stay-at-home dad) teaches Sunday school and serves on the nominating committee, and between preschool and the free church-sponsored child care offered during that aforementioned moms' group, my daughters are here nearly every day.

I recently joked that I have terrible boundaries. It's a risky joke to make in a profession riddled with stories of leaders who have destroyed trust and wounded innocents. I'll be very clear: despite the fact that in many denominations the language of "tending boundaries" has become

---

Rev. Katherine Willis Pershey is associate minister of First Congregational Church in Western Springs, Illinois. She previously served as solo pastor of South Bay Christian Church (Disciples of Christ) in southern California. She is author of *Any Day a Beautiful Change: A Story of Faith and Family*, and blogs at kewp. blogspot.com. She and her husband, Ben, have two daughters.

interchangeable with "preventing misconduct," I draw a rather large distinction between having porous, contextually appropriate boundaries and breaking sacred ones. A *monumental* distinction.

Still, the lack of compartments in my life does trespass against much of the conventional wisdom about boundaries and scrambles many of the traditional stereotypes about working motherhood. I'm not seeking that ever-elusive (mythological?) balance; instead, I have learned to embrace a messy but generally pleasant integration.

I do not merely tolerate the ways my personal and professional spheres are tangled. I enjoy the tangle. What has happened as I have slowly blurred the distinction between domestic life, writerly pursuits, and congregational work—as I've given up on maintaining separate calendars and instead jot "buy eggplant" right next to "write funeral liturgy" on my to-do list—is that I have stopped thinking of motherhood, ministry, and writing as roles I step in and out of, depending on whether I've tied on my apron, donned my stole, or sharpened my pencil. They are roles that I embody no matter what the context. I'm moving from *doing* (though there is still a lot of that) to *being*.

The upshot is that I feel remarkably authentic most days. I rarely pause to ponder what a pastor would do in any given situation. I just do what *I* would do, and that works, because I *am* a pastor.

As a writer and a lover of language, I think a lot about the words we use. The synonyms for *clergy* all have different connotations: *pastor, shepherd, preacher, minister, priest, cleric,* and, though it is technically not a noun, *reverend*. I've been hankering to bring back the word *parson*. As journalist Natalie Angier writes, "Etymology is ever the arbiter of truth,"* and so it is with *parson*. It traces its roots to the Latin *persona*, which originally referred to an actor's mask or a character in a play, but later came to mean "human being."

In many ways, being a pastor is simply being a person. A person who shows up, a person who prays, a person who worships, a person who sits at the table during really long council meetings.

Ministry is a generalist profession—what if it is so general that it is essentially to be a person of the church? And yet, ministry is also such that each parson—each *person*—is free to minister as him- or herself.

Some time ago, a parishioner confessed her frustration and anxiety about her husband's decision to embark on a rather plucky adventure in his retirement. I listened to her, and offered appropriate empathy and counsel, but in the course of the conversation the writer in me let that word slip out: *plucky*. And that word was grace to her. "I hadn't thought of him as 'plucky,'" she marveled. The word utterly transformed her view of her husband, and suddenly the burden of his adventure was far more bearable. I was tickled that it was not my pastoral sensibilities but my vocabulary that had been a source of healing.

There's no one right way to be a person, and there's no one right way to be a parson. I don't always respond in traditionally pastoral ways, but allowing myself to be the person/parson God created me to be works so much better than when I was more or less impersonating a pastor.

A version of this story appeared in *Fieldnotes Magazine*, a publication of the Max De Pree Center for Leadership.

* Natalie Angier, *Woman: An Intimate Geography* (New York: Houghton Mifflin, 1999), xvi.

Our Pheeto

Rev. Martha Spong

"What is that?"

RevGalBlogPals had a brand-new logo. The people in the know, our board members, were excited to debut it. A graphic artist designed it based on a story we shared. We got a .tiff and a .jpg to use on the web, but we were especially excited to have it on T-shirts.

"No, really. What is it?"

It seemed perfectly obvious to us. What else could it be?

"Is it an octopus?"

No.

Someone came a little closer.

"Is it a starfish?"

Actually, no. It's a circle of feet. Bare feet, rendered in bright colors, beside our organization's name in black. It was our first attempt at branding.

Pictures of feet, taken in a circle, date back to our beginnings. They are a way to mark a meet-up between bloggers without revealing the true identities behind their pseudonyms. The special beauty of the "pheeto" is you don't need an extra person to take the picture. You form a circle, and

---

Rev. Martha Spong is a United Church of Christ pastor and director of RevGal-BlogPals. She has served churches of many sizes and situations in Maine and Pennsylvania, specializing in intentional interim ministry. She writes prayers for pastors, adult curriculum, and preaching and liturgical resources, some of which she publishes at her blog, Reflectionary (marthaspong.com). Martha shares a manse full of books and yarn with her Presbyterian pastor wife, Rev. Kathryn Z. Johnston (also a contributor to *There's a Woman in the Pulpit*), and loves it when they have all four of their birds in the nest.

someone gets a picture from eye level while the rest of you lean out and try not to fall over.

My collection of pheetos includes meet-ups on city streets, on visits to mission work sites, and in my front yard. There are RevGals in sandals and sensible pumps and loafers and espadrilles. When I look through the pheetos, I remember what this RevGal and I had for lunch, wonder how that one is, or smile because I just talked to the other one yesterday.

When I, the blogger then known as Songbird, first met the blogger known as will smama, our two pairs of shoes were not enough for a circle, so we posed them in the grass outside the manse where she lived. She was a super-secret blogger, and while I had a more cavalier attitude about privacy, I blogged with a nickname for fun. In the picture, a pair of softball cleats, size 10, and a pair of lilac Crocs, size 5, sat side by side. It was the first of many pictures of our shoes, marking the beginning of an IRL (in real life) friendship between Kathryn (her real name) and me. Over many years, filled with countless emails and phone calls and pheetos, we supported each other through vocational changes and marital disillusionments. We counted back in amazement at the years we had known each other and came to treasure the person who owned the other pair of shoes.

At RevGals gatherings, we've taken pictures of feet in fancy shoes, and bare feet with fresh pedicures in and out of tropical waters, and even a collection of feet attached to ankles sporting tattoos, one real and the others airbrushed on for the duration of a cruise. Our gatherings grew so large that we realized we couldn't get all our feet in a picture at one time. We also recognized that it didn't matter as much anymore, because the blogosphere became less anonymous as bloggers realized people could figure out who they were anyway. We've become less protective of our real names and church locations.

Still, we keep taking these pictures. They have become a ritual of friendship. The image shape reminds us that we have formed a circle of friends around the country and around the world. We have the support of sisters in ministry around the clock, because someone somewhere is always awake. Pheetos trace our journey from anonymity to community, from budding cyber-friendships to lasting attachments.

Many pheetos later, Kathryn and I, now beyond nicknames, went to church to speak our covenant promises to each other. A professional photographer took the pictures, and as we grouped and regrouped with our children and the rest of our families and friends, we took one with the RevGals present. Six dear friends traveled from Texas, Mississippi, Delaware, and Pennsylvania to celebrate with us in Massachusetts. In the photo, all our faces shine with joy and perhaps a measure of wonder at what grew from that long-past meeting on a summer evening and two pairs of funny shoes in the grass. We looked elegant from head to toe, but the picture took us only from the knees up. We need another picture, someone said, and with a brief explanation to the photographer, we formed a circle of feet.

Perhaps it will seem like a strange artifact to our great-grandchildren. Perhaps no one will know whose feet were whose, that Kelly wore the high heels and Karla the patent-leather clogs. Maybe they will see the other photos and realize that my shoes were the black suede with a bow across the toe, and that Kathryn wore the smoking-hot boots that make her six feet tall.

"What is that?"

It's our pheeto. It's a picture of the people who stand with us.

Outside Over There

Moving in the World Beyond Our Churches

Go therefore and make disciples of all nations, baptizing them in the name of the Father and of the Son and of the Holy Spirit, and teaching them to obey everything that I have commanded you. And remember, I am with you always, to the end of the age.

MATTHEW 28:19–20

We are pastors, and we are twenty-first-century women. We thrive on caffeine, which means we buy skinny vanilla lattes at Starbucks, or maybe a chai at the local roastery. We knit, which means we shop and keep a stash of yarn. We run, which means we buy new shoes with frequency.

We take our kids to soccer or ballet or preschool, which means we wait, and while we wait we check Twitter or scan the nytimes.com headlines on our iPhones. We feed people, which means we write grocery lists and push carts through Wegman's and ponder the price of beer or diapers.

We live in the world, and at the same time we don't. Our calendar runs Monday to Sunday! Sunday! Sunday!—our goal line the entry into the sanctuary.

But Jesus never said, "Stay at church." When we focus too hard on that goal, we lose sight of the world outside our particular stadium. Then we wonder why the crowd has grown smaller, the cheering for our team diminished.

Hear, then, these stories from the faithful about the ways the wider world challenges and enriches the life of a pastor. Jesus sent us out to bring the good news to the world, but sometimes the world hands it right back to us and, when we least expect it, we find Jesus standing right beside us, outside over there.

What Are You Looking For?

Rev. Sarah E. Howe Miller, PhD

Innumerable days of ministry end with little or no resemblance to what was originally scheduled on the calendar. All too often, those days are not easily quantified, even though they are the essence of ministry. My antidote to those days is geocaching. When we started doing it, my then sixth-grade older daughter had no trouble labeling me "passionately obsessed."

Geocaching is a game played with a handheld GPS. Players set out to find a cache (container) hidden at a certain longitude and latitude, sign the log (a piece of paper) in the cache, and re-hide the container where it was found—without attracting attention. That is not always as easy as it sounds. The game requires enough focus to push the ever-spinning wheels of ministry concerns aside.

On the first-ever continuing education cruise by the RevGalBlogPals, known as the Big Event, I knew I would have the opportunity to extend my geocaching adventures into foreign territory. One find across the open seas and I would be an international geocacher. I lobbied for other adventurous souls to join me almost as soon as I arrived on board that huge

---

Rev. Sarah E. Howe Miller, PhD, is pastor of United Methodist Church of the Covenant in Arlington, Texas. Formerly, she was pastor of Epworth United Methodist Church in Arlington. Her doctoral dissertation is titled "Clergy-women and Grief: Local Church Pastors and Their Experience." Sarah blogs at thevicarofhogsmeade.wordpress.com. She loves to talk about geocaching and her two daughters, not necessarily in that order.

white ship. Three others had things they wanted to do that fit with wandering around to find geocaches: one wanted to collect sand, one wanted to find religious kitsch, and one simply wanted to put her feet in the water before getting back on board.

With all the experience of a rookie, I trusted myself more than my equipment. As the GPS continued to show us getting farther and farther from the one geocache I thought would be easy to find, and closer and closer to another more difficult one, I thought, *It's okay. We'll just find that one instead.* Of course, it never occurred to me that we were going the wrong way. An excursion that helped us discover the national park and some armed military guys but no geocache was not part of the plan, but I somehow managed to make that happen.

On the way back toward all the other tourists, I had the sinking feeling that I was not going to be an international geocacher. Then I saw a sign with a name familiar from the clues and I knew the cache had to be nearby.

There were four of us looking high and low in bushes and planters, around doorframes and windows, not really being too careful about being noticed because the excitement of a possible find took over. Suddenly, a guy walked past on the sidewalk and said, "More west."

"More west" led us down a short hallway that opened into an area filled with tables that had umbrellas instead of a ceiling over them, a pool with a swim-up bar, and steps that led to the Gulf of Mexico, where we promptly put our feet in the water. Finally, everyone but me had their requests fulfilled. The sidewalk guy saw us there and said, "You took the 'more west' kinda literally, didn't ya?" Knowing we were in the right vicinity gave us hope. We looked around the area for anything that might resemble a geocache.

Our earlier trek to "visit" the local national park and military base gave rise to thirst and hunger, so I offered to buy drinks; then we could go back to the ship for food and rest. As we waited to be noticed, someone got up to see if she could speed up the process. While trying to find someone to take a drink order, she noticed a mailbox and said, "Could it be the mailbox? Do they have mailboxes in Mexico?" After our drinks were served, I went over to the mailbox, looked at it, and reached up to open it. When I did, I yelled, like a soccer player scoring a goal, "*Yes!*"

We did much more than find a geocache that day. It was one of those moments when the whole is greater than the sum of the parts. At any point, my companions could have bailed, but they didn't. They could have made me feel "less than" on this crazy adventure that went awry, but they didn't. Even when I was trying to reconcile myself to extreme disappointment, they were still looking. I opened the mailbox, but the people I had only known by their blogging names—will smama, DogBlogger, and god_gurrlll—opened their hearts. I knew God had been walking with us, just as Jesus walked with the two friends on the road to Emmaus.

The find made me ecstatic.

The "walking with" made me blessed.

Soccer and Starbucks

Rev. Rachel G. Hackenberg

I lost two sanctuaries within the past year: the first to job relocation and the second to city planning. The temporary sanctuary currently filling my need for sacred and set-aside space is hardly shabby—it is surrounded by Italian marble and an indoor waterfall—but my spirit does not yet feel at home there. Although the faces and locations of each sanctuary have been different, all three boast the same values and bear the same name: Starbucks. Or—to its liturgically minded devotees—St. Arbucks.

Starbucks became a sanctuary space for me more than a decade ago when I needed a discreet space in which to confess to a friend that my marriage was hurtful and falling apart. There at a pale round table, under a solitary pendant light, caffeine in hand, my friend gave me permission to lament, to despair, to rage, and to believe that I was not alone.

Of course, we could have met in a church sanctuary, in the stillness of a sacred high-ceilinged space with only the ever-glowing red sanctuary lamp to witness our conversation. We could have sat together in a church office, with spines of theological books gazing silently at us while our stories unfolded. But all those spaces within church walls were work spaces for my friend and me—holy spaces, to be sure, but work spaces nonetheless, where professional deportment was required as we served to host safe and sacred space for congregants ... not for us.

Rev. Rachel G. Hackenberg is an author, United Church of Christ minister, and soccer mom. Her books include *Sacred Pause: A Creative Retreat for the Word-Weary Christian* and she blogs at faithandwater.com. Rachel currently serves on the national staff of the United Church of Christ.

So Starbucks became my safe and sacred space, my sit-and-be space, in a way that church could not be. At Starbucks, I could catch fifteen minutes of peace between dropping my kids at preschool and composing my spirit for the workday. I could schedule an occasional out-of-office "meeting" for myself simply to sit at Starbucks without interruption while my spirit wrestled before God. At Starbucks, I was safe to be tired, safe to be "off," safe to dream and imagine God's possibilities during a stressful life season.

St. Arbucks continued to provide sanctuary when I enrolled in seminary and, three years later, entered pastoral ministry. I began to invite congregants to Starbucks to experience and practice sanctuary beyond the church walls. Committee meetings and book groups and pastoral visits took place over cups bearing the green mermaid logo. As I introduced church members to the Starbucks sanctuary and built relationships with the Starbucks "regulars," my personal sanctuary space necessarily shifted. So the soccer field, where my two children practiced and played almost daily, became a much-needed quiet retreat for my spirit.

Soccer moms are not known for our quiet composure. Stereotypically, we outshout the coaches to tell our daughters and sons what to do on the field, while holding expensive lattes, sporting designer-label casual wear, and swapping local gossip. Over many years of attending my kids' games, I've heard soccer moms—and soccer dads—shout obscenities at ten-year-old players and at referees alike, and it's for good reason that many soccer programs institute a seasonal "quiet day" when parents must keep silent while watching their kids play.

I confess to fitting the soccer mom stereotype with my consumption of lattes (see Starbucks, above), but otherwise I am reclusive on the sidelines. Outdoors at a soccer practice or game, with the sun (or wind or snow or rain) on my face, I am content within a spacious natural sanctuary. At soccer, there is time to watch a red hawk soar lazily in the sky, time to listen to my own breath and heartbeat, time to witness the world without running at its pace, time to cheer on kids who are playing and working and maturing with every game. At soccer, I'm not asked to pray or preach or theologize or eulogize or respond to emails or shape a community's vision. I can simply be. I can be fully present—perhaps more present than I am in most other spaces. I can rest my spirit for ninety minutes.

Sanctuary is not stagnant or structural. Sanctuary is living and dynamic. My sanctuaries have had to move more often than I've changed home addresses. That first sanctuary I lost this year was my favorite Starbucks in the town where I pastored, which I left behind when I accepted a new ministry call in a new state. The second was the Starbucks that I was beginning to settle into in my new hometown, which was demolished to make way for a reconfigured intersection. My temporary Starbucks sanctuary is located inside a towering office building, next to an indoor atrium with a one-story waterfall. And my soccer sanctuary persists—week in and week out—wherever there is a sideline and a game. At each new juncture of life and ministry, I continue to learn that my sanctuary is any place where I can breathe and be, in quiet company with God.

The Body of Christ Shimmies

Rev. Marci Auld Glass

With trepidation, I walked into a dance studio full of women, wondering whose horrible plan it was to take a belly-dance class. *Oh, right. My plan.*

At least none of the women in the room knew me. And none of them knew my vocation. My yoga pants and sports bra were not liturgically colored. For once, my clergy status didn't walk before me into the room. And I wanted it to stay that way. So I could just be me, not the pastor me.

So many preconceptions travel with me when I walk into a room as a pastor. People expect me to be holy—or hypocritical. They hope I will pray for them or they pray I won't judge them. I'm never ashamed of being a clergywoman, but I confess that the weight of those preconceptions can weigh down my body and soul. When pastors wear stoles, the cloth bands symbolize the yoke, the weight of ministry. I understand that symbolism more now than I did when the installing pastor first placed the stole around my shoulders.

I've been dancing for a year now. I started out by setting the weight of my pastoral identity down by the door as I learned how to shimmy. And in the process, I've learned a lot about my self and my body.

Rev. Marci Auld Glass is pastor of Southminster Presbyterian Church in Boise, Idaho, and serves on the board of the Presbyterian Mission Agency. She blogs at marciglass.com and has written for numerous preaching resources. She enjoys belly dancing, craft bourbon drinking, and hiking in the Boise foothills with her family.

Before dance, I used to *have* a body. It carried my brain around, which was its primary task. It enjoyed a good meal. It enjoyed some pleasures, for sure. But before dance, I'm not sure I was ever fully present in my body. I once ran a half marathon and did a triathlon, but those activities were largely motivated by a desire to lose weight so I could continue to eat what I wanted.

Belly dance has given me an appreciation for being embodied. Dancing is fun. It can also be maddening and frustrating, but overall, it is just plain fun. And there is a gift in perseverance, in practicing week after week and finally seeing change as your brain and body work together to learn new things.

I used to spend more time than I want to admit in wishing I had another body—a less voluptuous body, a smaller-waisted body, one with better knees. The animosity I felt toward my body contributed to the disconnect I felt between my self and my body, I'm sure.

But to dance, you have to ask your body to do new things, to do difficult things. Why would my body want to do that for someone who loathed it and wished it were something else? Dancing has helped me appreciate the "skin I'm in" and has taught me to love and appreciate my embodied self. My hips can do five different kinds of shimmy! My belly can roll and undulate! My shoulders can shimmy and pop! And because mine is more voluptuous than a photoshopped magazine-model's body, I actually have flesh that you can see move as it shimmies and shakes!

As I dance, I feel grounded and present in my body. I also feel much lighter and joy-filled. And as I've become more comfortable in my own embodied self, I've been able to better bear the weight of my pastoral identity. My fellow dancers now know I'm a pastor. But they knew me first as the person struggling next to them to learn something new, to try something different, and to live into her self. I also experience my self differently as I step into the pulpit each week, feeling that groundedness and presence, realizing it isn't just my mind engaging with the congregation as I preach, but all of my self.

As I've worn my pastoral identity more intentionally with my dancing, I've also considered our call, as Christians, to be the body of Christ. Can we, as the church, allow the disconnect between body and self to continue? If we are the body of Christ, does the body of Christ struggle with eating disorders? Does the body of Christ feel self-loathing and hatred? Does the body of Christ wish it were some other body? Or does the body of Christ find joy in being exactly who it is? Does the body of Christ embrace itself, flaws and all, as beautiful and created with joy? Does the body of Christ root itself in its own community and context, present in the world where God has placed it?

For my part, I'm working to make sure the body of Christ shimmies.

At the Barn

Rev. Laurie Brock

"Quit being pushy!" I heard my riding instructor yell as I struggled to ride Cowboy. He was pulling against his reins. I was pulling back. I was trying to slow down his trot. He was breaking into a canter. We were not getting along.

Much like Spanx, putting on a particular role is often far easier than peeling it away inch by inch. I had been wearing the role of Mother Laurie, rector, for the past few days, as I organized, planned, listened, and grieved. One of my parishioners, a retired priest, had died after a long illness. Clergy funerals are a particular kind of insanity. At this one, all the usual grief and liturgically organized mourning were accompanied by a bishop preaching and officiating at the funeral, a slew of clergy in other roles, and a sit-down dinner for over two hundred—the wishes of the deceased. As rector, I was in charge of organizing all this, which necessitated some pushiness to get everything accomplished.

Cowboy was, in his perfect horsey way, letting me know that I needed to return to my deepest self and soul and leave all the Mother Laurie stuff back at the church. Because I wasn't at the church anymore. I was at the barn.

Rev. Laurie Brock is rector at Saint Michael the Archangel Episcopal Church in Lexington, Kentucky, and formerly served Episcopal churches in Alabama and Louisiana. She is author of *Where God Hides Holiness* and blogs at dirtysexyministry. com. When Laurie isn't letting horses teach her about God, she enjoys exploring historical sites in Kentucky, often ones that include bourbon distilleries, and wondering why there isn't a reality show about fabulous clergywomen.

The barn. That place where the ancient scents of horse, hay, and mud return me to my incarnate self. When I sit on the back of a horse, I give my soul time to catch up to my body, which often, in the life of ministry, moves at a pace far too fast and insane for our souls to keep up. Under the guidance of a horse, I give myself time to quit being pushy, worried about the budget, far too organized for the next youth event, or completely unprepared for Sunday's sermon, and to start being more present to the whole person of Laurie and not just Mother Laurie, Episcopal priest.

Books and class discussions are excellent entrées into the vocation and profession of ministry, but in the master class of ordained ministry, we delve into the deepest aspects of ourselves. This spiritual formation often occurs in surprising places, during life-altering events, and with much wiser teachers than we are. For that, God needs horses—at least for me.

Horses are some of the most breathtaking animals in God's creation. They know my feelings and thoughts before I do and force me, in their way, to face them without words. Horses are a perfect reflection of a person's soul. If you are nervous and anxious, they respond with their own anxiety. To calm a skittish horse, you must tap into your inner calm. To collect an excited horse, you must first collect yourself. Horses communicate through physical senses rather than words, so they force riders to be aware of what we are saying through our bodies.

All too often, we humans think we can avoid our feelings. When asked how we feel, when we are upset, angry, or disjointed, we say, "Fine." We intellectualize our emotions, giving them rational explanations when they may be a swirling miasma that can't be explained with words. We even think we must select what we are feeling instead of accepting that we feel conflicting emotions all at once.

These behaviors are, quite honestly, lies to our selves and souls, and horses call us on these lies. We cannot lie about our feelings. We cannot read a book to intellectualize our way out of them. Horses demand that we experience what we are feeling in our bodies, selves, and souls if we are going to work together.

The church and even our congregations often expect us to act a certain way, to not express our anger, frustration, disappointment, or sadness. In other words, we are supposed to deny the deepest soil of human emotion because we are clergy. Not a particularly helpful lesson or practice.

The wisdom of horses is that by spending time with and honoring those emotions, I can experience them being transformed, released, or simply understood. "Feel them in your skin and bones," the horse asks, as we walk around the ring. "Trust that what you need, you will keep, and what you don't need, I'll ask you to lose," the horse tells me as we move between gaits.

I dropped my shoulders, loosened my fingers, and felt the reins give. Cowboy moved his head forward, just to see if I had finally listened to him. I sat deep in the saddle and felt him respond by slowing his gait. Within a few feet, we went from fighting each other to being a melded team, trotting and cantering around the ring with calm focus. An hour of riding later, I was hot, with a fine layer of horse hair mixed with the sweat on my skin. The tension in my shoulders, where the weight of ministry settles, had dissipated somewhere during the ride, cast off into the shavings and dirt of the ring.

Cowboy nuzzled me as I walked him back to the barn, reminding me of the peppermints I keep in my pocket. While pushiness wasn't something I needed anymore, Cowboy was quite certain that quality in him would be rewarded with a treat.

He was right about that too.

No Masks

Rev. Martha Daniels

It can be hard for me to *not* be a pastor, but I need that relaxation, that time to express and remember the parts of me that aren't used much in my ministry: my love of historical literature, my interest in steam railroads, my joy in cooking and gardening. I want to share all of me with friends and family, and that's why we have friends (or should) outside the congregation. It's easy to drop the clergy mask with my close family; but friends with whom I can do that are rarer and highly valued.

My nonchurch friends are a blessing (and every pastor should have at least one). There is no need or tendency to "talk shop" with them; I can share with them things I cannot share with the congregation. With these friends, I can drop the mask and discuss pretty much anything that isn't church-related—the latest crime novel from a favorite writer, the best place to find fresh strawberries, the political goings-on in town.

One of those friends called me one day and said, "We've started a trivia team and I think you should be on it." I wasn't doing anything that night and had wanted to get together with her anyway, so I agreed and went along.

Rev. Martha Daniels is senior pastor of Metropolitan Community Church of Windsor in Windsor, Ontario, and previously was a pastoral intern at MCC–Washington, D.C. She is author of "Not Even on the Page: Freeing God from Heterocentrism," an article published in the *Journal of Bisexuality*. She blogs at rainbowpastor.blogspot.com. She is a bibliophile with a special interest in the historical fiction of Dorothy Dunnett and Patrick O'Brian, and all the historical rabbit trails down which they lead her.

The trivia night was held at one of the local pubs. Each team was given an answer booklet for the fill-in-the-blank music questions and multiple-choice questions, plus a sheet of images to identify. There was also a bonus question, which you found out by checking the pub's Facebook page that day. Questions ranged from "What was the pen name of Charles Dodgson?" to "How many pro football teams do not have plural names?" We always found the music to be the hardest part—given a five-second snippet of a song (never the chorus, of course), we had to name the song and the artist. The images ranged from photos of cars to product labels with the words removed to flags of obscure countries—all of which we had to identify.

We called ourselves "The Small but Mighty," because we started out with only three members, and most teams had the full six allowed by the rules. We began to think strategically, recruiting a couple of new members who were experts on geography, biology, and contemporary music. We picked up a pro tip from the team that usually sat next to us, and began writing our answers on notepads and showing them to each other, rather than shouting them out, which might give a competitor help. Our strategies worked, and while we are not shoo-in winners every week, we usually place among the top three.

Recently, the format has changed to include swag prizes. I am now the proud (?) owner of a red glass beer boot and a one-liter beer mug, emblazoned with the lyrics to the Canadian national anthem. It must have been a Canada Day promotion.

Now most Wednesday nights you will find me at the pub, sharing a plate of nachos, sipping a local lager, laughing and discussing possible answers to the questions. Looking around, I see people staring at the ceiling, their lips moving—trying to remember the next line of the song, which *surely* has the title in it. Others scribble furiously on their notepads, showing suggestions to their teammates as the scribe nods and begins to write the answer in the booklet. The team next to us, the pinnacle team, the perennial champions—who are really nice people—look over to catch our eyes and chuckle as another impossible-to-recognize song plays. Afterward, we spill out into the parking lot, laughing with glee at getting some answers right, annoyed with ourselves for missing ones we really did know.

Trivia night is two hours weekly to be myself, without being on the alert for possible pastoral needs or for where the church is needed in the community. It's where I can truly relax and slip off all those masks of leader, teacher, spiritual guide. I don't mean that I am only pretending to be those things, but there are ways of acting, being, and speaking that go with those roles that don't express all of me. Those masks, while necessary, can also be suffocating.

For those two hours, I can be all of me. It's part of my self-care—to open myself up and remember that I am more than pastor and community worker. Those two hours give me the space I need to give voice to the facets of me that aren't expressed in ministry. My obscure knowledge of railroads, gardening, and literature is needed and respected in that time and place—all of me, no masks.

Out of the Pool

Rev. Katya Ouchakof

When I started going to water aerobics classes in my late twenties, I had knee problems and needed the low-impact workout. A few years later, my knees were much better, but I kept going because it offered a good workout and I liked the people—the other regulars and the instructors. During this time I was a candidate for ordination in the Evangelical Lutheran Church in America. The community at the gym was helpful, since the people welcomed me unconditionally at a time when it felt that my welcome in the church was conditional on my candidacy process. When my ordination was delayed and I started considering other options, I thought, *I could teach these classes.* When the eight-year-long process finally resulted in my ordination, those thoughts fell by the wayside.

About a year later, I was learning what all new pastors have to figure out: how to do good self-care and keep boundaries between professional and personal life. Then the gym started advertising for new water aerobics instructors. I figured that teaching classes at the gym could help me get away from the church sometimes, and would require me to work out regularly. So I applied, and was enthusiastically hired by Mary, one of the longtime instructors.

Rev. Katya Ouchakof is an ELCA pastor serving in the South-Central Synod of Wisconsin. She is author of a handful of book reviews, dozens of devotional materials, and countless sermons, some of which can be found at Proclamation (canoeistpastor.blogspot.com). She enjoys canoeing and kayaking, watching *Star Wars* movies, and playing board games with her husband.

Teaching at the gym was a great way to get to know people outside of church. While most of the other instructors and regular class participants knew that my "day job" was as a pastor, they didn't treat me any differently than they treated the other instructors. Occasionally, someone would come to me with a prayer request, but I was not by any means the pastoral caregiver in that group.

Until, one day, I was.

Tracy, one of Mary's closest friends, was a longtime instructor who had been battling cancer for over a year. When Tracy became so ill that she couldn't teach anymore, Mary would keep the instructors informed about her condition, because, inevitably, the regulars would ask. They were concerned. We had become our own close, supportive community.

I showed up to teach one morning and found the gym's overnight manager still on duty, waiting for me. He had taken a call from Mary early that morning. Tracy had died during the night.

In my life as a chaplain and pastor, I had walked with many families through times of illness and times of grief. This time, however, was different: I wasn't the pastor to this group of people; I was one of them. As a class participant, I had admired Tracy as an instructor. I had only been teaching for a few months, and I was still in awe of her expertise. But now it was my job to break the news of Tracy's death to a pool full of class members who loved and respected her.

Somehow we all made it through class that day. It wasn't so much that Tracy's death was unexpected, since we knew she was doing poorly. But the last thing most people want to do after receiving bad news is have a kick-butt workout. Yet we made it work. And then I went home and called Mary. I asked her if she knew what the family was planning, if there was a date or location for the funeral, or if they needed any help. I said something like, "I don't want to insert myself where I'm not needed, but remember that this is what I do as my day job. So if there's any way I can help, let me know."

Later that day, Mary called me back. She had talked with Tracy's sister and brother, and they wanted me to do the funeral. They both lived out of town and Tracy hadn't belonged to a church in years, so they were grateful for my help.

Over the next few days I did that most sacred work of funeral planning with the family. When the day arrived, I dressed in my usual black suit. Several of the class regulars showed up for the funeral. Half of them didn't recognize me at first—we looked different in real clothes, instead of in our swimsuits! After the service, they put the pieces together. They were glad that the person who had led the funeral was someone who had known Tracy in real life. And I was glad that I had been able to serve the community in this way.

After the funeral, life went back to normal at the pool. We kept an orchid in Tracy's memory until it stopped blooming. I received a few comments about the service when I showed up to teach. But over time, we all got used to our new normal. And, as a member of that community, I discovered that being a pastor can be a way to serve God's people at large.

Saint Paul versus Danielle Steele

Rev. Amber Belldene

Long before I became a romance writer, one of my favorite priestly duties was to preach at weddings. I loved to get to know a couple and to tell their mostly secular family and friends about the miracle of their love—the ways it was full of grace; the ways it challenged them; the ways it was an icon of God's love for humanity, shining outward brightly for us to see.

I also love the description of marriage in the Episcopal Book of Common Prayer as meant for "mutual joy." Whether a person is religious, spiritual, or a secular humanist, anyone with a body knows that phrase alludes to sex, among other shared pleasures. As an ordained person, it feels to me profound to proclaim this gloriously sexy—and sometimes also awkward—spiritual truth: romantic and erotic love are sacramental. Sexual pleasure is a divine gift. It's a radical message, especially to people who expect the church to be either silent or damning on the subject. Mature romantic love is not saccharine or simple, but a discipline that leads us to transcendence.

As a young woman exploring sexuality, my primary texts were the Bible and romance novels, and they ran in my head side by side. Saint

---

Rev. Amber Belldene is a romance novelist and the alter ego of an Episcopal priest with a full-time and semisecret church job. She is the author of the Blood Vine series, blogs at amberbelldene.com, and did not even blush when, at a diocesan clergy conference last year, her wonderful bishop told her he'd read her racy debut novel.

Paul endorsed married, straight sex as a stopgap measure for those who couldn't handle celibacy until the second coming. Romances were the stories of people whose desire and connection to each other were so strong they could overcome immense internal and external obstacles to love.

I am very glad I didn't only have Saint Paul. Romance novels taught me that passion, mutual pleasure, and that kind of ecstasy were things to seek out. They taught me that my desires and the physical expression of affection were good—holy even—and nurtured an inkling that Saint Paul was wrong about some things. He was right about a lot, but he didn't give us a perfect recipe for sexual ethics in modern life. The truth is, since the beginning the church has failed at putting forward a sexual ethics for everyday life. Our tradition has not acknowledged the holy and hard work of being a sexually whole person.

When I was twenty-three, my ordination process was put on hold because I was unmarried and living with my now-husband, though I had been honest about our cohabitation and the work we were doing to prepare for marriage. I felt deeply ashamed. The message was clear: as long as my sex life was invisible, it was okay. No one seemed to think I was doing anything wrong, it just wasn't holy enough for a priest. Except, of course, that doesn't make any sense. The faithful work of being a whole human in a reconciled relationship with others *is* holy.

After my wedding, I was made a candidate for Holy Orders and subsequently ordained, but I did not forget the institution's discomfort with sexuality—mine or anyone's. The church is rightly focused on the noble goal of sexual abuse prevention, yet, out of fear and a tradition of neglecting this fraught subject, we are largely silent about the goodness of sex. Meanwhile, our culture, for both good and ill, becomes more sexually explicit and permissive.

I write and read romance novels because they have helped me find wholeness. They are smart, fun, passionate romps, which have taught me about love and all the ways it can heal and redeem. Although I write under a pen name, I'm public about being a priest because I want to be a voice in claiming the holy, hot spiritual goodness of human sexuality.

I began writing romance with trepidation, fear for my career, and shame about being a publicly sexual person, all of which lingered from my ordination process (as if my children were immaculately conceived). But, thankfully, I have received great support from colleagues and superiors. Since I started speaking out about the connectedness of sex and spirituality, I have found that both secular and religious people are starving for this conversation. Once, at a romance readers' convention, someone asked me how writing racy books and being a priest go together. I said, "Very well, because God loves Love." To my surprise, the room burst into applause.

Since then, I have had people contact me via Facebook for pastoral sex advice because they don't know any clergy they can talk to, or to confide that their pastor condemned romance novels from the pulpit and they felt ashamed because they experienced those books as life-giving. I have met people who did not know there were Christians who celebrated sexuality. Each time something like this happens, I become a little more free of my lingering shame about my own sexuality, and more sure of my pursuit of writing about love and sex as a complementary vocation.

People long for the good news that their mutual joy in erotic love is a taste of divine blessing. When a clergyperson proclaims this truth, God's wanton love for humanity becomes a little more accessible. And that's why I write romance novels.

I Am Grateful
A Prayer

Rev. Karla Miller

In this vast and brilliant world,
I am grateful
for the barista who makes my iced Americano perfectly,
for the clerk who helps me find the perfect Shiraz to take to
    a party,
for the lunch ladies at school who survive four lunch
    periods and recess every day.

In this cold and silent world,
I am grateful
for the last leaf clinging to a maple tree in the dead of
    winter,
for the shimmers of light and night at dusk,
for the single-minded barking of the neighbor's dog at
    midnight.

Rev. Karla Miller is a United Church of Christ pastor who knows the truth about cats and dogs, as she and her spouse, Liz, have opened their home in a Boston suburb to many rescues. She blogs at Amazing Bongoes (karlajeanmiller.blogspot.com). Her interests include art, people, politics, social issues, pocketbooks, shoes, shoes, chocolate, hiking, running, early evening when the sun is getting tired, discovering new music, playing with clay, and the Boston Red Sox.

In this busy and rushing world,
I am grateful
for the man holding a sign in the traffic circle, asking for
    spare change,
for the accidental jostling in the crowded aisle at the grocer,
for singing off-key with wrong words to pop songs with
    children on the way to school.

Your presence dazzles, Holy God, in every moment.
In the cup we share,
the bread we break,
the struggle of table fellowship,
the tenacity of hope,
the cry of struggle,
the joy of community,
the song of life.

For all the ways in which you teach us to be faithful,
in all the living of our ordinary days,
we give you thanks.
Amen.

Learning in the Shipyard

Rev. Liz Crumlish

Every week as a child, I clambered up scaffolds, crawled through make-shift tunnels, meandered in and out of corridors, cupboards, and cub-byholes. I witnessed the formation of giant chambers that would contain the massive buoys to mark the shipping channels along the Western Isles of Scotland. Now, twenty years later, I finally learned what a "hold" was and could comprehend how my dad had been partially disabled by falling down one such gaping hole—still an ever-present hazard in this hostile workplace of modern ship construction. At the time, my twin brother and I were simply amused to see our dad, both legs in casts, sit and bump his way up and down the stairs in our home. We were too young to take in how it could have cost him his life, how terrifying it must have been for both our parents.

All these years later, I frequented a shipyard very similar to the one where my dad spent most of his working life, even after his accident. The Church of Scotland funds posts so that people are cared for pastorally at their places of work. Mine was a part-time position alongside parish ministry because the shipyard was within the bounds of the parish. I spent time hanging out with the craftsmen, some of whom had been called out of retirement to practice and pass on to another generation their skills in crafting ornate wooden rails and other necessary items of ships' fittings and furniture.

Rev. Liz Crumlish is a Scottish Presbyterian minister living and working on the west coast of Scotland. She has worked as a hospital chaplain and now serves as a parish minister. She loves to spend time walking on the beach, processing thoughts and writing in her head, with the stunning scenery of Scotland as a backdrop.

Summer had given way to autumn and then winter and now, in the harshness of this gray December day, at last some warmth was to be filtered into the marrow of these tough, unyielding men of steel (and they were all men) with whom I had journeyed on my weekly early-morning visits to their place of work.

Never mind all the pomp and circumstance surrounding a royal visit. This was their day, their moment of pride. And, by association, perseverance, and grudging acceptance, I was to be allowed to take on a tiny part of that ownership. For I, too, had huddled around braziers, sipping tea from filthy mugs that I learned not to examine too closely. I, too, in my steel-toed shoes and hard hat, had slipped on the ice of the dock on frosty mornings and learned to avoid the lure of the hungry holds when I clambered aboard. I was a mere girl to these men who had "kent my faither [known my dad]," but they accepted me as one of their own.

So it was that on this December day I took my place on the platform, sick to the core with nerves, but clinging tenaciously to my badge of office and simply making up the rest as I went along. I was presented to Her Majesty Queen Elizabeth and His Royal Highness Prince Philip, promptly forgetting, in my anxiety, the protocol briefing about forms of address and handshakes. But this was my slot in the proceedings. Nothing else could happen until I had blessed this vessel that the queen was about to launch. Remembering the succinct advice of the men who had greased the ways to "keep it short," I read some scripture and pronounced a blessing on this testament to almost-forgotten skills, giving thanks for the workforce whose fruit this was, and seeking protection for the future. Only then could her majesty press the button and release the champagne, as she pronounced the name of "our" ship—*MV Pharos*, a Northern Lighthouse Board vessel.

There was frenzied activity as the stocks were knocked out and then a sharp intake and holding of breath. The *Pharos* paused theatrically before her first movement, and then quickly gathered momentum, careering down the ways and crashing resoundingly into the water. "We" had done it again. This, the last of the lower Clyde shipyards, had produced a beauty and we knew it. Even the shipyard chaplain was allowed to bask in that glory!

And so, another liturgy was written on the fly, informed by the need to minimize the time the ship waited on the well-greased stocks, another privilege of ministry was exercised, and all manner of things were taught to a fledgling chaplain by men with calloused hands and choice phrases and hearts of gold, wrapped up in wisdom and grace.

But that was not the end of the story. A few days later, *Lloyds List*, an eminent shipping journal published in London, carried a story lamenting how times had changed in the seafaring world. The article noted that it once was the case that if a fisherman on his way to his boat should even catch sight of a woman, it was considered an unfortunate omen. Yet now in Scotland, a woman had blessed a ship before the vessel's launch.

Changed days indeed. Days blessed by the wonder and unpredictable nature of ministry exercised alongside the least likely teachers we encounter every day.

Who I Am
Is Not What I Did

Rev. Julie Craig

It's cocktail party patter. Neighborhood potluck chitchat. "What do you do?" the other person asks.

Because we all know it is the *doing* that matters.

In the midst of a life transition, that question is the one that makes my blood run cold, the one that makes my palms sweaty—even for a second— the one that makes my head swim momentarily. The one that makes my heart skip a beat, and not in a good way.

While adrenaline has a field day with my insides, I stammer slightly on the outside, always catching my breath before I attempt an answer. I tend to answer the question somewhat differently every time it is asked. I have friends who work in law enforcement, but always claim to be florists. I haven't yet thought of an answer as clever and unexpected as that one.

I am transitioning out of life as a pastor. And separating the *doing* and the *being* is sometimes a chore. Especially when doing and being are so intricately interwoven that it's hard to tell where one leaves off and the

---

Rev. Julie Craig is a writer, speaker, preacher, ordained teaching elder in the Presbyterian Church (USA), and graduate of San Francisco Theological Seminary. She and her spouse live in Pewaukee, Wisconsin, while their grown children carry on just fine without them in far-flung places. A failed knitter, reluctant dog walker, and capricious reader, she is fueled by strong coffee, deep laughter, and really cute shoes.

other begins. Like when doing and being are the conjoined twins in the life of pastoral ministry.

I recall all those sermons, all those times I talked publicly about not just *doing* church but *being* church. I talked about preaching the gospel at all times and in all places, even without words, about living a life that reflects the grace and love and hope and generosity of Christ, and I asked people to do this out in public, in their everyday lives—in their work and at play and at home.

And for all I know, some of them did.

Now the person who must learn to do this is me, for I do not have the office of pastoral ministry to lean on. I do not have the institutional church, and my authority within it, to hide behind.

I recently was at a regional event held at a church. A large sign above the door in the narthex leading to the parking lot proclaimed, *You are now entering the mission field!* I remember proclaiming that very hope myself, in a charge at the end of worship that began with "Go out into the world ..."

Well, this is the world and I am out in it.

What I do and who I am are no longer conjoined twins. It has taken me some time, but I have slowly and deliberately untangled those twisted, helical strands of vocation and identity. I no longer approach life and the world from the perspective of how I earn a paycheck, and I find that my world has expanded, for I no longer have to connect everything with everything else. Those engaged in pastoral ministry do this, whether or not we admit it or notice it or acknowledge it. We seek to tie a trip to the supermarket, a conversation with the church administrator, an encounter at the town library with the texts we are preaching. We read a story online or in a novel or watch it unfold on the screen and wonder if it will fit with the Sunday school lesson we are preparing. The search for meaning and connection never ends.

Suddenly, being out in the world means I no longer have to look for the hidden puzzle piece that will pull everything together by Saturday night. A trip to the supermarket is just an errand to buy broccoli and chicken. My everyday conversations no longer end up in a sermon or a Sunday school lesson, for which I am sure my family and friends are grateful. I am freed up to enjoy films knowing that I won't have to find the "God moments" if I don't want to. (Though I often still do.)

Lest I sound too cheery at the thought of stepping away from the privilege and responsibility of parish ministry, I acknowledge that there is loss in my current situation. There is loss of community and loss of connection. I have mourned the fact that I am no longer part of something that is concretely changing a tiny corner of the world in the way that small local churches and their ministries do.

And yet this is the world and I am out in it. There is still a gospel to proclaim, and a life that begs to be lived, reflecting the grace and love and hope and generosity of Christ, God willing. There is still being and still doing, even if the one is not so bound to the other as to make them indistinguishable.

Perhaps the most indelible lesson I have learned is not to get caught up in the habit of trying to get to know others—truly know and understand them at their core, their being—by asking them the dreaded obvious cocktail party question. Because doing and being don't *always* intersect in obvious ways.

But this: "Tell me about yourself ..."

I think that will do.

The Priest I Want to Be

Rev. Sara Irwin

I've been an Episcopal priest for ten years. I will be the first to say it: this is not a normal job. There's no nine to five, and I don't know how to quantify billable hours out of making theology from the last movie I saw or checking pregnant parishioners' Facebook pages for birth announcements. My "part-time" clergy friends work full time, and the full-time ones work all the time. My best image (and favorite part) of congregational ministry is that I get to be like a crow, scavenging ideas and metaphors and moments of God working in the world.

This idea hit me most powerfully when I came across performance artist Marina Abramović's retrospective "The Artist Is Present," at the Museum of Modern Art in New York. A sequence in it became the center of a sermon, but even later, I couldn't get her out of my head. I didn't just want to use her ideas. I wanted to *be* her. Marina Abramović the artist is the priest I want to be.

In her piece, Abramović sat at a table for eight hours a day for three months, while museumgoers could come and sit opposite her. She sat absolutely still.

I saw a documentary about her preparation for the work—especially striking as I was getting ready for Holy Week, the days leading up to Easter

---

Rev. Sara Irwin is just another radical feminist lady priest mama serving at Christ Church Episcopal in Waltham, Massachusetts. She previously served as associate rector at Emmanuel Church in Boston. She is author of the title story in *My Red Couch and Other Stories on Seeking a Feminist Faith*. Her blog is at saraiwrites. blogspot.com. She loves all things outdoorsy and progressively political.

Sunday that recall Jesus's journey of crucifixion and resurrection. Episcopal liturgy *does* Holy Week—we cheer with palms at the processional on Sunday, we wash feet on Thursday remembering Jesus's last supper with his friends, we stare in horror at the cross on Good Friday. And on Easter, we're raised too. As with the resurrection of Jesus, wherever you fall in the spectrum between metaphor and literal resuscitation is between you and God. Either way, the work takes time.

Peering down the days from Palm Sunday, I know Easter is coming, but I also know there's still a long way to go before we're there. When Abramović talks about her preparation, it's physical as well as spiritual. The self and the piece merge, but also split each other open to create something new. She says that the artist has to be a warrior, undertaking unreasonable feats of endurance with no part of the self left aside. I long for this fierce sense of confidence and commitment, but I also recognize that sometimes being split open and poured out is a lot less romantic than Abramović makes it sound. When my children need to be fed and I'm too tired to even articulate a preference for Indian over Chinese food for dinner, I don't feel very warrior-like. But this is how real vocation works— the artist, the priest, the writer, the activist (and, yes, the parent); these endeavors are not optional.

In her piece at MoMA, as each person came to sit with her, Abramović offered her singular gaze. In seeing each person, she opened a space for that one to see himself or herself reflected there in wholeness and integrity, in love and patient acceptance. She *saw* each person, with all of her being.

As best I can tell, that's what the work of God is, and the work of God we are called to take part in. The *imago dei*, the image of God in each of us that is so singular and lovely and precious and longing to be seen—it's our holy calling to see and be seen. Even as we live our lives pretending we are only our own, even as the detritus of prejudice, malice, greed, and self-hatred can obscure our holy nature, that image of God is still there. The holy gaze is also impersonal, showing that we are each loved no more, but—crucially—no less, than anyone else. Nothing is required of us. Most of the people who sat at Abramović's table had the same reaction: they cried. Whether from relief or comfort or fury or fear, the response was the same as when I pick up my four-year-old after a hard day. When someone sees you, really sees you, it's safe to fall apart. The places in contemporary life where that is true are not many.

So every year I gaze toward Easter, beginning the journey from Palm Sunday. Every year the liturgies are part performance, part spectacle, all prayer. Every year I try to see each person, try to inhabit each step toward the cross. I can fear this walk we undertake, from death into life. I can resist it. I can do it well or poorly, preach coherent and lovely sermons or fall apart. The grace, though, for the priest (as well as the artist) is that in front of the altar, all of that comes along, and none of it matters. You can have feelings *about* the future or the past. But you can only inhabit the singular moment. You can only be present, seeing and being seen, offering what you have and receiving what God returns.

For Some Reason

Rev. Stephanie Anthony

On my way to pastor appreciation chapel at my daughter's preschool, I texted a good friend. *It's been a no-fun day—not bad, just no fun—but it's about to get better.*

My daughter's school is the preschool-through-eighth-grade ministry of a church that doesn't practice the ordination of women. When the invitation was delivered to the area ministerial association, I set a reminder on my phone; if it worked out for me to go, I would go, but I wasn't going to make any Herculean effort to be there. For some reason, though, when the alert went off, I decided to put down everything and head out the door.

You seem to enjoy poking bears with sticks, my friend texted in return, and, to some degree, he is right. There are seventeen different Christian congregations in our ministerial association. Only five could even call women as pastors if they wanted to. And I make a habit of finding subtle ways to point out the patriarchy around me.

Six of my (male) colleagues stood in the narthex when I arrived. Heads snapped in my direction as I joined the circle, but the host pastors greeted me warmly. After gathering my daughter from her classroom, I found a seat in the sanctuary.

Rev. Stephanie Anthony is pastor at First Presbyterian Church in Hudson, Wisconsin. She previously served as associate pastor of First Presbyterian Church in Lincoln, Nebraska. Her blog, She Rev Writes, can be found at sherev.blogspot. com. When not poking bears with sticks, she is usually spending time with her husband, Phil, and children, Karoline, William, and Margaret in the purple sparkly dress.

A sixth grader came forward to read a poem on the theme of the service, a poem about the holy men who so faithfully heard and obediently followed the call to be pastors. The little hairs on the back of my neck began to tickle. As the boy returned to his seat, the congregation's youth director bounded onstage, opening his sermon by asking the students what they wanted to be when they grew up. *A teacher! An architect! A nurse!* I whispered the question to my own daughter in my lap. "You know that, Mom," she said. "A beautiful princess in a purple sparkly dress." She's right; I knew.

The youth director continued preaching, asking all the pastors who were present to stand so that he could come to us and let us introduce ourselves. The small voice beside me squeaked, "Pastors, Mom! That's you! Stand up!" I stood.

The youth director moved through the pews, bringing the microphone. He passed me once, to start with one of the pastors of the church in which we were worshipping. Understandable. He passed me a second time, maybe to get to another pastor with whom the children were more familiar. However, when he passed by me a third time without so much as a glance, and then continued on with his message, having talked to every other standing pastor except for me, my face began to redden with frustration and embarrassment.

"Why didn't he talk to you, Mama?"

I was just about to sit down when both of my colleagues from the host congregation interrupted the youth director, pointing out that he missed one of the pastors in the room. Hoping my voice didn't sound as uneasy as it felt, when the microphone came to me, I proudly introduced myself. When I sat down, my daughter crawled back in my lap, whispering in my ear, "You're a pastor too."

I tried to listen to the rest of what was said, but I'll admit it wasn't easy. Maybe I should have anticipated what happened; when you choose to poke bears with sticks you have to know that they might poke back. But I always hope for a little more, like the little more I got when my two colleagues stood up and made sure I was included in the recognition.

Finally, the youth director invited all the students to find a pastor in the room and lay hands on them for prayer. I worried I would be left out again. I focused my attention on my daughter, who asked if she could play with her dress-up liturgical stole when we got home.

Then I felt the first touch, a small hand on my shoulder. Looking up, I saw it belonged to a young girl, maybe a fifth grader. Three or four more girls came in my direction, followed by a couple of younger boys. By the time the prayer started, they surrounded me.

For some reason that afternoon I had left my desk, worship unplanned and Sunday school lessons not yet written, and now I saw this was it. It wasn't to be honored, nor to be appreciated. It wasn't even just to poke the bear with a stick. I came because God called me to my church and this community. I was called to show my little girl, and all the girls and boys whose hands were weighing down my body, heavy with blessing and responsibility, that God could be calling them too.

Running with Patience

Rev. Julia Seymour

There are all kinds of bodies at the start of a race. My body is never one of the ones in front. Sleekly dressed, timers primed, race snacks in streamlined pouches, the front-of-the-pack people impress me. I admire them, but I do not even aspire to be one of them. They are not me.

The middle-of-the-pack people at the starting line jog in place. They wear shirts advertising other races. Their shoes are worn and comfortable. They have their own records to beat, their own pace to keep. They are competitive in a friendly way. The middle-of-the-pack people always offer encouragement to those they pass on the trail. I like these people and hope to become one. Right now, they are not me.

Those of us shuffling nervously at the back of the pack have a variety of motivations. We are sticking with friends, adhering to resolutions, trying something new. There are veterans in the back of the pack, including me, who hang there so that we do not slow the pace of others. The back of the pack, this cluster of bodies, is my people. They are me.

I am short. I am about fifty pounds overweight. I do not have a running habit. I love to enter 5K races, marathons, mountain scrambles, and

---

Rev. Julia Seymour has been the ordained minister at Lutheran Church of Hope in Anchorage, Alaska, since August 2008. She believes strongly in ecumenical and interfaith cooperation. She blogs at lutheranjulia.blogspot.com. Julia enjoys reading, writing, crochet, and outdoor activities. She lives with her husband, their two young children, and their devoted Labrador retriever.

triathlons. I have my own rules—challenging myself, improving my time, and running across the finish line no matter what else happens. I spend a lot of time, money, and effort to be at the back of the pack.

It occurs to me, as I gasp and pound through the race, that I have never bought a gadget to keep track of how many minutes I pray a day. I do not assiduously log the time I spend reading scriptures or commentaries. I have never set goals for myself with regard to spiritual discipline.

Even at the back of the pack in a race, I am working to improve my results. Embarrassed, I confess to never applying that philosophy to my devotional life. Admitting that is painful. The reality, of course, is that between text studies, adult education, children's chapel, and weekly sermons, I do not feel like I have time or energy, much less desire, for additional time with the word or in silence.

The three thousand daily steps that accumulate through work, family life, errands, and chores around the house are never steps that I count toward my exercise goals. By the same logic, the general accrual of time with the Bible, and praying when called on, probably should not figure in my accumulated devotional time.

The front-of-the-pack spiritual people are people I admire. They write their own prayers. They draw pictures or plant gardens or rake sand. They meditate—inhaling grace, exhaling peace. Even in their dark nights of the soul, their candles still give light to others. I admire them. I must learn to accept that I do not have to be one of them.

The middle-of-the-pack people share their struggles—in conversations, blogs, articles. They are able to maintain steady disciplines. They focus on tangible objects and see depth and beauty. Their devotional life seems easy and fulfilling for them. They offer encouragement to others. I hope to become one of these, but I am not there yet.

I am currently at the back of the pack of devotional life. My prayers are harried and come in spurts throughout the day. Moments of quiet are not planned, but occur before I fall into an exhausted sleep. My devotional reading of scripture has no schedule, no plan. God has brought me into this race, but I have not yet found a rhythm.

If I am willing, as a fairly unathletic person, to devote significant time, money, and energy to physical races, why don't I do the same for my spiritual life? I have to try things out, discarding what doesn't work and shaping what does into something that specifically helps me. My race goals are challenging myself, improving my time, and running across the finish line, no matter what else happens. Surely those translate, in some capacity, to my spiritual practice.

With racing, I just had to make up my mind to commit to it and do it. With my devotional life, with praying, with spiritual disciplines, I have to do the same. Of course, I have access to the same Trainer as the people in the front of the pack and the middle of the pack. Even now, she whispers, "Let's get moving."

Acknowledgments

RevGalBlogPals has been a collaborative effort from the beginning, the work of people drawn together by a common urge toward community despite great geographical distance. This book began the same way, with half a dozen women video-chatting from their homes and offices in Scotland, Massachusetts, Pennsylvania, Kansas, Wisconsin, Idaho, and Alaska. My great thanks to Julie Craig, Liz Crumlish, Marci Auld Glass, Joanna Harader, Karla Miller, Julia Seymour, and Julie Woods, all of whom helped write material included in the book proposal and brainstorm the themes of the book. Thank you to all the writers who have expressed a slice of the diverse lives and personalities that make up RevGalBlogPals.

Thanks also to RevGal Rachel G. Hackenberg, who shared her expertise in writing and publishing by encouraging me as well as reading the manuscript before submission, and Carol Howard Merritt, who first suggested that RevGalBlogPals could become a platform for sharing the voices of clergywomen with the world. Thanks to Rev. Michael Kirby, who encourages all RevGals to "be fierce and fabulous for Jesus." Thanks to Mary Beth Butler, who puts the BlogPal in RevGals: "We made a thing, and it is awesome!"

I am grateful to Emily Wichland at SkyLight Paths Publishing for suggesting we do this book, to Rachel Shields for her thoughtful guidance, and to everyone else at SkyLight Paths for their faithful and creative work.

And at my house, thank you to my wife, Kathryn Z. Johnston, who made sure I always had coffee; to our son Will who would get home from school just in time to say hi to the RevGals on video-chat; and to our grown-up children, Edward, Peter, and Lucy, who offered encouragement via text and Skype.

Thanks be to God for these incredible gifts.

Inspiration

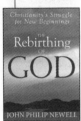

Deepening Engagement
Essential Wisdom for Listening and Leading with Purpose, Meaning and Joy
By Diane M. Millis, PhD; Foreword by Rob Lehman
A toolkit for community building as well as a resource for personal growth and small group enrichment.
5 x 7¼, 176 pp, Quality PB, 978-1-59473-584-4 **$14.99**

The Rebirthing of God
Christianity's Struggle for New Beginnings
By John Philip Newell
Drawing on modern prophets from East and West, and using the holy island of Iona as an icon of new beginnings, Celtic poet, peacemaker and scholar John Philip Newell dares us to imagine a new birth from deep within Christianity, a fresh stirring of the Spirit.
6 x 9, 160 pp, HC, 978-1-59473-542-4 **$19.99**

Finding God Beyond Religion: A Guide for Skeptics, Agnostics & Unorthodox Believers Inside & Outside the Church
By Tom Stella; Foreword by The Rev. Canon Marianne Wells Borg
Reinterprets traditional religious teachings central to the Christian faith for people who have outgrown the beliefs and devotional practices that once made sense to them.
6 x 9, 160 pp, Quality PB, 978-1-59473-485-4 **$16.99**

Fully Awake and Truly Alive: Spiritual Practices to Nurture Your Soul
By Rev. Jane E. Vennard; Foreword by Rami Shapiro
Illustrates the joys and frustrations of spiritual practice, offers insights from various religious traditions and provides exercises and meditations to help us become more fully alive.
6 x 9, 208 pp, Quality PB, 978-1-59473-473-1 **$16.99**

Perennial Wisdom for the Spiritually Independent
Sacred Teachings—Annotated & Explained
Annotation by Rami Shapiro; Foreword by Richard Rohr
Weaves sacred texts and teachings from the world's major religions into a coherent exploration of the five core questions at the heart of every religion's search.
5½ x 8½, 336 pp, Quality PB, 978-1-59473-515-8 **$16.99**

Journeys of Simplicity: Traveling Light with Thomas Merton, Bashō, Edward Abbey, Annie Dillard & Others *By Philip Harnden*
5 x 7¼, 144 pp, Quality PB, 978-1-59473-181-5 **$12.99**

Saving Civility: 52 Ways to Tame Rude, Crude & Attitude for a Polite Planet
By Sara Hacala 6 x 9, 240 pp, Quality PB, 978-1-59473-314-7 **$16.99**

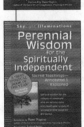

Spiritually Healthy Divorce: Navigating Disruption with Insight & Hope
By Carolyne Call 6 x 9, 224 pp, Quality PB, 978-1-59473-288-1 **$16.99**

Prayer / Meditation

Calling on God
Inclusive Christian Prayers for Three Years of Sundays
By Peter Bankson and Deborah Sokolove
Prayers for today's world, vividly written for Christians who long for a way to talk to and about God that feels fresh yet still connected to tradition.
6 x 9, 400 pp, Quality PB, 978-1-59473-568-4 **$18.99**

The Worship Leader's Guide to Calling on God
8½ x 11, 20 pp, PB, 978-1-59473-591-2 **$9.99**

Openings, 2nd Edition
A Daybook of Saints, Sages, Psalms and Prayer Practices
By Rev. Larry J. Peacock
For anyone hungry for a richer prayer life, this prayer book offers daily inspiration to help you move closer to God. Draws on a wide variety of resources—lives of saints and sages from every age, psalms, and suggestions for personal reflection and practice. 6 x 9, 448 pp, Quality PB, 978-1-59473-545-5 **$18.99**

Openings: A Daybook of Saints, Sages, Psalms and
Prayer Practices—Leader's Guide 8½ x 11, 12 pp, PB, 978-1-59473-572-1 **$9.99**

Men Pray: Voices of Strength, Faith, Healing, Hope and Courage
Created by the Editors at SkyLight Paths; With Introductions by Brian D. McLaren
Celebrates the rich variety of ways men around the world have called out to the Divine—with words of joy, praise, gratitude, wonder, petition and even anger—from the ancient world up to our own day.
5 x 7¼, 192 pp, HC, 978-1-59473-395-6 **$16.99**

Honest to God Prayer: Spirituality as Awareness, Empowerment,
Relinquishment and Paradox *By Kent Ira Groff*
6 x 9, 192 pp, Quality PB, 978-1-59473-433-5 **$16.99**

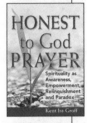

Lectio Divina—The Sacred Art
Transforming Words & Images into Heart-Centered Prayer
By Christine Valters Paintner, PhD
5½ x 8½, 240 pp, Quality PB, 978-1-59473-300-0 **$16.99**

Sacred Attention: A Spiritual Practice for Finding God in the Moment
By Margaret D. McGee 6 x 9, 144 pp, Quality PB, 978-1-59473-291-1 **$16.99**

Secrets of Prayer: A Multifaith Guide to Creating Personal Prayer in Your Life
By Nancy Corcoran, CSJ 6 x 9, 160 pp, Quality PB, 978-1-59473-215-7 **$16.99**

Women of Color Pray: Voices of Strength, Faith, Healing, Hope and Courage
Edited and with Introductions by Christal M. Jackson
5 x 7¼, 208 pp, Quality PB, 978-1-59473-077-1 **$15.99**

Prayer / M. Basil Pennington, OCSO

Finding Grace at the Center, 3rd Edition: The Beginning of
Centering Prayer *With Thomas Keating, OCSO, and Thomas E. Clarke, SJ*
Foreword by Rev. Cynthia Bourgeault, PhD A practical guide to a simple and beautiful form of meditative prayer. 5 x 7¼, 128 pp, Quality PB, 978-1-59473-182-2 **$12.99**

The Monks of Mount Athos: A Western Monk's Extraordinary
Spiritual Journey on Eastern Holy Ground *Foreword by Archimandrite Dionysios*
Explores the landscape, monastic communities and food of Athos.
6 x 9, 352 pp, Quality PB, 978-1-893361-78-2 **$18.95**

Psalms: A Spiritual Commentary *Illus. by Phillip Ratner*
Reflections on some of the most beloved passages from the Bible's most widely read book. 6 x 9, 176 pp, 24 full-page b/w illus., Quality PB, 978-1-59473-234-8 **$16.99**

The Song of Songs: A Spiritual Commentary *Illus. by Phillip Ratner*
Explore the Bible's most challenging mystical text.
6 x 9, 160 pp, 14 full-page b/w illus., Quality PB, 978-1-59473-235-5 **$16.99**
HC, 978-1-59473-004-7 **$19.99**

Retirement and Later-Life Spirituality

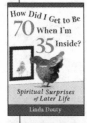

Caresharing
A Reciprocal Approach to Caregiving and Care Receiving in the Complexities of Aging, Illness or Disability
By Marty Richards

Shows how to move from independent to *inter*dependent caregiving, so that the "cared for" and the "carer" share a deep sense of connection.

6 x 9, 256 pp, Quality PB, 978-1-59473-286-7 **$16.99**; HC, 978-1-59473-247-8 **$24.99**

How Did I Get to Be 70 When I'm 35 Inside?
Spiritual Surprises of Later Life
By Linda Douty

Encourages you to focus on the inner changes of aging to help you greet your later years as the grand adventure they can be.

6 x 9, 208 pp, Quality PB, 978-1-59473-297-3 **$16.99**

Soul Fire
Accessing Your Creativity
By Thomas Ryan, CSP

This inspiring guide shows you how to cultivate your creative spirit, particularly in the second half of life, as a way to encourage personal growth, enrich your spiritual life and deepen your communion with God.

6 x 9, 160 pp, Quality PB, 978-1-59473-243-0 **$16.99**

Restoring Life's Missing Pieces
The Spiritual Power of Remembering & Reuniting with People, Places, Things & Self
By Caren Goldman; Foreword by Dr. Nancy Copeland-Payton

Delve deeply into ways that your body, mind and spirit answer the Spirit of Re-union's calls to reconnect with people, places, things and self. A powerful and thought-provoking look at "reunions" of all kinds as roads to remembering the missing pieces of our stories, psyches and souls.

6 x 9, 208 pp, Quality PB, 978-1-59473-295-9 **$16.99**

Creative Aging
Rethinking Retirement and Non-Retirement in a Changing World
By Marjory Zoet Bankson

Explores the spiritual dimensions of retirement and aging and offers creative ways for you to share your gifts and experience, particularly when retirement leaves you questioning who you are when you are no longer defined by your career.

6 x 9, 160 pp, Quality PB, 978-1-59473-281-2 **$16.99**

Creating a Spiritual Retirement
A Guide to the Unseen Possibilities in Our Lives
By Molly Srode

Retirement can be an opportunity to refocus on your soul and deepen the presence of spirit in your life. With fresh spiritual reflections and questions to help you explore this new phase.

6 x 9, 208 pp, b/w photos, Quality PB, 978-1-59473-050-4 **$14.99**

Keeping Spiritual Balance as We Grow Older
More than 65 Creative Ways to Use Purpose, Prayer, and the Power of Spirit to Build a Meaningful Retirement
By Molly and Bernie Srode

As we face new demands on our bodies, it's easy to focus on the physical and forget about the transformations in our spiritual selves. This book is brimming with creative, practical ideas to add purpose and spirit to a meaningful retirement.

8 x 8, 224 pp, Quality PB, 978-1-59473-042-9 **$16.99**

Spiritual Practice—The Sacred Art of Living Series

Teaching—The Sacred Art: The Joy of Opening Minds & Hearts
By Rev. Jane E. Vennard Explores the elements that make teaching a sacred art, recognizing it as a call to service rather than a job, and a vocation rather than a profession. 5½ x 8½, 160 pp, Quality PB, 978-1-59473-585-1 **$16.99**

Conversation—The Sacred Art: Practicing Presence in an Age of Distraction
By Diane M. Millis; Foreword by Rev. Tilden Edwards, PhD
5½ x 8½, 192 pp, Quality PB, 978-1-59473-474-8 **$16.99**

Dance—The Sacred Art: The Joy of Movement as a Spiritual Practice
By Cynthia Winton-Henry 5½ x 8½, 224 pp, Quality PB, 978-1-59473-268-3 **$16.99**

Dreaming—The Sacred Art: Incubating, Navigating & Interpreting Sacred Dreams
for Spiritual & Personal Growth *By Lori Joan Swick, PhD*
5½ x 8½, 224 pp, Quality PB, 978-1-59473-544-8 **$16.99**

Fly-Fishing—The Sacred Art: Casting a Fly as a Spiritual Practice
*By Rabbi Eric Eisenkramer and Rev. Michael Attas, MD; Foreword by Chris Wood, CEO,
Trout Unlimited; Preface by Lori Simon, executive director, Casting for Recovery*
5½ x 8½, 160 pp, Quality PB, 978-1-59473-299-7 **$16.99**

Giving—The Sacred Art: Creating a Lifestyle of Generosity
By Lauren Tyler Wright 5½ x 8½, 208 pp, Quality PB, 978-1-59473-224-9 **$16.99**

Haiku—The Sacred Art: A Spiritual Practice in Three Lines
By Margaret D. McGee 5½ x 8½, 192 pp, Quality PB, 978-1-59473-269-0 **$16.99**

Hospitality—The Sacred Art: Discovering the Hidden Spiritual Power of Invitation
and Welcome *By Rev. Nanette Sawyer; Foreword by Rev. Dirk Ficca*
5½ x 8½, 208 pp, Quality PB, 978-1-59473-228-7 **$16.99**

Labyrinths from the Outside In, 2nd Edition
Walking to Spiritual Insight—A Beginner's Guide *By Rev. Dr. Donna Schaper and
Rev. Dr. Carole Ann Camp* 6 x 9, 208 pp, b/w illus. and photos, Quality PB, 978-1-59473-486-1 **$16.99**

Lectio Divina—**The Sacred Art**
Transforming Words & Images into Heart-Centered Prayer
By Christine Valters Paintner, PhD 5½ x 8½, 240 pp, Quality PB, 978-1-59473-300-0 **$16.99**

Pilgrimage—The Sacred Art: Journey to the Center of the Heart
By Dr. Sheryl A. Kujawa-Holbrook 5½ x 8½, 240 pp, Quality PB, 978-1-59473-472-4 **$16.99**

Practicing the Sacred Art of Listening
A Guide to Enrich Your Relationships and Kindle Your Spiritual Life
By Kay Lindahl 8 x 8, 176 pp, Quality PB, 978-1-893361-85-0 **$18.99**

Recovery—The Sacred Art: The Twelve Steps as Spiritual Practice *By Rami Shapiro*
Foreword by Joan Borysenko, PhD 5½ x 8½, 240 pp, Quality PB, 978-1-59473-259-1 **$16.99**

Running—The Sacred Art: Preparing to Practice *By Dr. Warren A. Kay*
Foreword by Kristin Armstrong 5½ x 8½, 160 pp, Quality PB, 978-1-59473-227-0 **$16.99**

The Sacred Art of Chant: Preparing to Practice
By Ana Hernández 5½ x 8½, 192 pp, Quality PB, 978-1-59473-036-8 **$16.99**

The Sacred Art of Fasting: Preparing to Practice
By Thomas Ryan, CSP 5½ x 8½, 192 pp, Quality PB, 978-1-59473-078-8 **$15.99**

The Sacred Art of Forgiveness: Forgiving Ourselves and Others through God's Grace
By Marcia Ford 8 x 8, 176 pp, Quality PB, 978-1-59473-175-4 **$18.99**

The Sacred Art of Listening: Forty Reflections for Cultivating a Spiritual Practice
By Kay Lindahl; Illus. by Amy Schnapper 8 x 8, 160 pp, b/w illus., Quality PB, 978-1-893361-44-7 **$16.99**

The Sacred Art of Lovingkindness: Preparing to Practice
By Rabbi Rami Shapiro; Foreword by Marcia Ford 5¼ x 8¼, 176 pp, Quality PB, 978-1-59473-151-8 **$16.99**

Spiritual Adventures in the Snow: Skiing & Snowboarding as Renewal for Your Soul
By Dr. Marcia McFee and Rev. Karen Foster; Foreword by Paul Arthur
5½ x 8½, 208 pp, Quality PB, 978-1-59473-270-6 **$16.99**

Thanking & Blessing—The Sacred Art: Spiritual Vitality through Gratefulness
By Jay Marshall, PhD; Foreword by Philip Gulley 5½ x 8½, 176 pp, Quality PB, 978-1-59473-231-7 **$16.99**

Writing—The Sacred Art: Beyond the Page to Spiritual Practice
By Rami Shapiro and Aaron Shapiro 5½ x 8½, 192 pp, Quality PB, 978-1-59473-372-7 **$16.99**

Professional Spiritual & Pastoral Care Resources

Change & Conflict in Your Congregation (Even If You Hate Both)
How to Implement Conscious Choices, Manage Emotions & Build a Thriving Christian Community *By Rev. Anita L. Bradshaw, PhD* Positive, relational strategies for navigating change and channeling conflict into a stronger sense of community. 6 x 9, 176 pp, Quality PB, 978-1-59473-578-3 **$16.99**

Professional Spiritual & Pastoral Care
A Practical Clergy and Chaplain's Handbook
Edited by Rabbi Stephen B. Roberts, MBA, MHL, BCJC
An essential resource integrating the classic foundations of pastoral care with the latest approaches to spiritual care, specifically in acute care hospitals, behavioral health facilities, rehabilitation centers and long-term care facilities.
6 x 9, 480 pp, HC, 978-1-59473-312-3 **$50.00**

Spiritual Guidance across Religions
A Sourcebook for Spiritual Directors & Other Professionals Providing Counsel to People of Differing Faith Traditions
Edited by Rev. John R. Mabry, PhD
This comprehensive professional resource offers valuable information for providing spiritual guidance to people from a wide variety of faith traditions. Covers the world's major faith traditions as well as interfaith, blended and independent approaches to spirituality. 6 x 9, 400 pp, HC, 978-1-59473-546-2 **$50.00**

College & University Chaplaincy in the 21st Century
A Multifaith Look at the Practice of Ministry on Campuses across America
Edited by Rev. Dr. Lucy Forster-Smith; Foreword by Rev. Janet M. Cooper Nelson
Examines the challenges of the secular context of today's college or university campus.
6 x 9, 368pp, HC, 978-1-59473-516-5 **$40.00**

Disaster Spiritual Care
Practical Clergy Responses to Community, Regional and National Tragedy
Edited by Rabbi Stephen B. Roberts, MBA, MHL, BCJC
and Rev. Willard W. C. Ashley, Sr., MDiv, DMin, DH
The definitive guidebook for counseling not only the victims of disaster but also the clergy and caregivers who are called to service in the wake of crisis.
6 x 9, 384 pp, HC, 978-1-59473-240-9 **$50.00**

How to Be a Perfect Stranger, 6th Edition
The Essential Religious Etiquette Handbook
Edited by Stuart M. Matlins and Arthur J. Magida
The indispensable guidebook to help the well-meaning guest when visiting other people's religious ceremonies. Covers: **African American Methodist Churches • Assemblies of God • Bahá'í Faith • Baptist • Buddhist • Christian Church (Disciples of Christ) • Christian Science (Church of Christ, Scientist) • Churches of Christ • Episcopalian and Anglican • Hindu • Islam • Jehovah's Witnesses • Jewish • Lutheran • Mennonite/Amish • Methodist • Mormon (Church of Jesus Christ of Latter-day Saints) • Native American/First Nations • Orthodox Churches • Pentecostal Church of God • Presbyterian • Quaker (Religious Society of Friends) • Reformed Church in America/Canada • Roman Catholic • Seventh-day Adventist • Sikh • Unitarian Universalist • United Church of Canada • United Church of Christ**
6 x 9, 416 pp, Quality PB, 978-1-59473-593-6 **$19.99**
"The things Miss Manners forgot to tell us about religion."
—*Los Angeles Times*

Caresharing: A Reciprocal Approach to Caregiving and Care Receiving in the Complexities of Aging, Illness or Disability *By Marty Richards*
6 x 9, 256 pp, Quality PB, 978-1-59473-286-7 **$16.99**; HC, 978-1-59473-247-8 **$24.99**

Learning to Lead: Lessons in Leadership for People of Faith
Edited by Rev. Williard W. C. Ashley Sr., MDiv, DMin, DH
6 x 9, 384 pp, HC, 978-1-59473-432-8 **$40.00**

The Perfect Stranger's Guide to Funerals and Grieving Practices
A Guide to Etiquette in Other People's Religious Ceremonies
Edited by Stuart M. Matlins 6 x 9, 240 pp, Quality PB, 978-1-893361-20-1 **$16.95**

Women's Interest

There's a Woman in the Pulpit: Christian Clergywomen Share Their Hard Days, Holy Moments & the Healing Power of Humor
Edited by Rev. Martha Spong; Foreword by Rev. Carol Howard Merritt
Offers insight into the lives of Christian clergywomen and the rigors that come with commitment to religious life, representing fifteen denominations as well as dozens of seminaries and colleges. 6 x 9, 240 pp, Quality PB, 978-1-59473-588-2 **$18.99**

She Lives! Sophia Wisdom Works in the World
By Rev. Jann Aldredge-Clanton, PhD
Fascinating narratives of clergy and laypeople who are changing the institutional church and society by restoring biblical female divine names and images to Christian theology, worship symbolism and liturgical language.
6 x 9, 320 pp, Quality PB, 978-1-59473-573-8 **$18.99**

Birthing God: Women's Experiences of the Divine
By Lana Dalberg; Foreword by Kathe Schaaf
Powerful narratives of suffering, love and hope that inspire both personal and collective transformation. 6 x 9, 304 pp, Quality PB, 978-1-59473-480-9 **$18.99**

Women, Spirituality and Transformative Leadership
Where Grace Meets Power
Edited by Kathe Schaaf, Kay Lindahl, Kathleen S. Hurty, PhD, and Reverend Guo Cheen
A dynamic conversation on the power of women's spiritual leadership and its emerging patterns of transformation.
6 x 9, 288 pp, Quality PB, 978-1-59473-548-6 **$18.99**; HC, 978-1-59473-313-0 **$24.99**

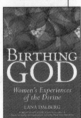

Spiritually Healthy Divorce: Navigating Disruption with Insight & Hope
By Carolyne Call A spiritual map to help you move through the twists and turns of divorce. 6 x 9, 224 pp, Quality PB, 978-1-59473-288-1 **$16.99**

Bread, Body, Spirit: Finding the Sacred in Food
Edited and with Introductions by Alice Peck 6 x 9, 224 pp, Quality PB, 978-1-59473-242-3 **$19.99**

Dance—The Sacred Art: The Joy of Movement as a Spiritual Practice
By Cynthia Winton-Henry 5½ x 8½, 224 pp, Quality PB, 978-1-59473-268-3 **$16.99**

Daughters of the Desert: Stories of Remarkable Women from Christian, Jewish and Muslim Traditions *By Claire Rudolf Murphy, Meghan Nuttall Sayres, Mary Cronk Farrell, Sarah Conover and Betsy Wharton*
5½ x 8½, 192 pp, Illus., Quality PB, 978-1-59473-106-8 **$16.99** Inc. reader's discussion guide

The Divine Feminine in Biblical Wisdom Literature
Selections Annotated & Explained
Translation & Annotation by Rabbi Rami Shapiro; Foreword by Rev. Cynthia Bourgeault, PhD
5½ x 8½, 240 pp, Quality PB, 978-1-59473-109-9 **$18.99**

Divining the Body: Reclaim the Holiness of Your Physical Self
By Jan Phillips 8 x 8, 256 pp, Quality PB, 978-1-59473-080-1 **$18.99**

Honoring Motherhood: Prayers, Ceremonies & Blessings
Edited and with Introductions by Lynn L. Caruso
5 x 7¼, 272 pp, Quality PB, 978-1-58473-384-0 **$9.99**; HC, 978-1-59473-239-3 **$19.99**

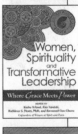

New Feminist Christianity: Many Voices, Many Views
Edited by Mary E. Hunt and Diann L. Neu
6 x 9, 384 pp, Quality PB, 978-1-59473-435-9 **$19.99**; HC, 978-1-59473-285-0 **$24.99**

Next to Godliness: Finding the Sacred in Housekeeping
Edited by Alice Peck 6 x 9, 224 pp, Quality PB, 978-1-59473-214-0 **$19.99**

The Triumph of Eve & Other Subversive Bible Tales
By Matt Biers-Ariel 5½ x 8½, 192 pp, Quality PB, 978-1-59473-176-1 **$14.99**

Woman Spirit Awakening in Nature: Growing Into the Fullness of Who You Are
By Nancy Barrett Chickerneo, PhD; Foreword by Eileen Fisher
8 x 8, 224 pp, b/w illus., Quality PB, 978-1-59473-250-8 **$16.99**

Women of Color Pray: Voices of Strength, Faith, Healing, Hope and Courage
Edited and with Introductions by Christal M. Jackson 5 x 7¼, 208 pp, Quality PB, 978-1-59473-077-1 **$15.99**

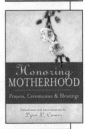

About SKYLIGHT PATHS Publishing

SkyLight Paths Publishing is creating a place where people of different spiritual traditions come together for challenge and inspiration, a place where we can help each other understand the mystery that lies at the heart of our existence.

Through spirituality, our religious beliefs are increasingly becoming a part of our lives—rather than *apart* from our lives. While many of us may be more interested than ever in spiritual growth, we may be less firmly planted in traditional religion. Yet, we do want to deepen our relationship to the sacred, to learn from our own as well as from other faith traditions, and to practice in new ways.

SkyLight Paths sees both believers and seekers as a community that increasingly transcends traditional boundaries of religion and denomination—people wanting to learn from each other, *walking together, finding the way.*

For your information and convenience, at the back of this book we have provided a list of other SkyLight Paths books you might find interesting and useful. They cover the following subjects:

Buddhism / Zen	Gnosticism	Poetry
Catholicism	Hinduism / Vedanta	Prayer
Chaplaincy		Religious Etiquette
Children's Books	Inspiration	Retirement & Later-Life Spirituality
Christianity	Islam / Sufism	
Comparative Religion	Judaism	Spiritual Biography
	Meditation	Spiritual Direction
Earth-Based Spirituality	Mindfulness	Spirituality
	Monasticism	Women's Interest
Enneagram	Mysticism	Worship
Global Spiritual Perspectives	Personal Growth	

Or phone, fax, mail or email to: SKYLIGHT PATHS Publishing
Sunset Farm Offices, Route 4 • P.O. Box 237 • Woodstock, Vermont 05091
Tel: (802) 457-4000 • Fax: (802) 457-4004 • www.skylightpaths.com
Credit card orders: (800) 962-4544 (8:30AM–5:30PM EST Monday–Friday)
Generous discounts on quantity orders. SATISFACTION GUARANTEED. Prices subject to change.

**For more information about each book,
visit our website at www.skylightpaths.com.**